Materiality and Society

Materiality and Society

Tim Dant

Open University Press

Open University Press
McGraw-Hill Education
McGraw-Hill House
Shoppenhangers Road
Maidenhead, Berkshire
England SL6 2QL

email: enquiries@openup.co.uk
world wide web: www.openup.co.uk

and Two Penn Plaza, New York, NY 1012–2289
USA

First published 2005

A catalogue record of this book is available from the British Library

ISBN 0 335 20855 X (pb)   0 335 20856 8 (hb)

Library of Congress Cataloging-in-Publication Data
CIP data has been applied for

Typeset by BookEns Ltd, Royston, Herts.
Printed and bound in Great Britain by
CPI Group (UK) Ltd, Croydon, CR0 4YY

To Mollie – who showed me that there is
more to material interaction than
working on her car

Contents

Preface

We spend much of our waking time more or less alone, not interacting with anyone. But we are always living with the things that have been produced within our society, things which have a cultural resonance that makes the flow of our lives feel familiar, just as much as the sound of our language does. At work, at rest, at play, whether other people are involved or not, material things accompany the activities of our body and provide the environment for everything we do. And in the world of the second millennium, for most of us, these material things are human made, shaped or placed in accord with the conventions of our culture – whether it is the trees in the local park or the arrangement of furniture in an office. As a sociologist interested in theoretical ideas and as a social policy researcher interviewing all sorts of different types of people – usually the least well-off in our society – I began to realize that much of what society gives to people that is useful, is stuff. It is the material environment of homes and workplaces and all the things in them that shape the context in which our personal lives of loves and ambitions are played out. Now although this has always been the case, material life has for long periods of history been relatively stable with new types of objects or technologies being introduced relatively slowly. In earlier times, our material environment was much more shaped by nature and our response was oriented by need rather than choice. But at the turn of the twenty-first century what seems to be of constant interest and concern to us is the stuff that surrounds us, that we use and that we live in and among.

In the past it was religious beliefs, a sense of shared pride in nationality or a common ideology that gave a society its identity. In the late modern world it is as likely to be the shared difficulties we have in moving about our society or in getting the mundane things of life to work properly, that give us a sense that we share the world. What all humans have in common is our sense of embodiment, which means that whatever our many differences, we know that we have at least similar practical experiences of the material world we live in. In an earlier book *Material Culture in the Social World* (Open University Press, 1999), I explored a number of the ways in which this commonality of embodied experience shapes society. I argued that it was not simply in consuming, if that means buying, acquiring or appropriating things, that material culture was meaningful to us. I suggested that it was through the mundane ways in which we interact with things that our material culture becomes partly constitutive of our social worlds. In this book I want to take that idea further and explore how the realm of the material has become tied up with our ideas about what society is and in particular to start to unravel some of the fundamental, but taken-for-granted, ways that we interact with things. There is a running example of the car – a type of object that so many of us interact with so often and that seems to shape our societies in many ways. But, with the help of a research grant and a colleague, I took this example a little further by studying rather closely how those who repair and maintain cars actually do interact with a material object. This was a practical type of material interaction to study; cars are big objects that stay in one place when they are being worked on and, while the work practices of a repair garage were strange to us as researchers, much of what went on was largely familiar and comprehensible through out own limited technical understanding of cars. The technicians were engaged in skilled work that is of great significance in our society (after all, they keep our cars running ...) yet it is essentially a particular form of the type of material interaction that we all engage in as we use objects and tools in our everyday life.

At home using kitchen or other domestic equipment, at the office using pens, filing cabinets, computers, and telephone and in all sorts of work and leisure activities, we use things to shape the world around us and enable us to do what we need or wish to do in it. As we manipulate objects to affect other objects they become 'tools' and many of the objects we encounter we co-opt as instruments to realise our ends in the world. In this sense the work of the car technicians is an exemplar of our everyday interaction with objects and this is the reason for discussing it in this book. The technicians' material interaction with the underneath workings of our cars is a sustained form of the sort of material interaction in which we all engage with a wide range of different types of objects – including the car that we drive. Now the material stuff, the objects, that we encounter in our ordinare lives are just about all products of our culture and our society; they have been shaped for instrumenetal purposes and designed to fit in with particular types of cultural practice. As we use them to shape our lives and ralise our intentions and goals, so they shape us, guiding us in the ways of our society. The consequence is that how we act on the world is entailed inthe objects made available to us in our partricular cultural context. Our actions take the form of physical force – it might be as slight as the pressing of a button or speaking an instruction to a sensing device – that has effects in the material world around us. But what we do in the material word is shaped in two ways" firt, by the direct impact of objects on our perceptions channelled via the bodily sensations of sight, touch, smell, taste and sound; and second, the meanings and significance of these bodily sensations are shaped through the embodied processes of mind and memory by our cultural experience. However much our reflective conscousness is brough to bear, however much we feel we are acting through our wone ill, our actions are constrained by the material objects to hand and the cultural experience we have acquired. Often what do is routine, habitual and hardly guided by thought so we follow a culturally acquired practice that accords with the materiality of the objects with which we are confronted. Together with the discursive and political realtionships between people, which are more usually the domain of sociology, our material interactions, whether conscious or habitual, both manifest and realize the culture of the society in which we live. If you think that interacting with things is not important to you, just try to remember the last time that you were *not* engaged in some sort of 'material interaction'.

I would especially like to thank David Bowles who was the research associate on the ESRC project on 'Car Care: The Repair and Maintenance of the Private Car' (R00023370) that was undertaken at the University of East Anglia during 2000/1. David was behind the camera for the video work and undertook the great majority of the fieldwork. He was also very involved in drafting reports and early project papers – but most importantly he enjoyed discussing what we could see on the video recordings and trying to make sense of the process of material interaction. I would like also to thank all those who took part in the project, including managers, proprietors and members of the advisory group but, most importantly, the technicians who generously allowed us to watch and record them at work.

My special thanks must go to Bernadette Boyle for her kind help with the translations from French. I would also like to thank Jon Hindmarsh, Christian Heath and Dirk vom Lehn at the Work, Interaction and Technology Research Group at King's College, London. They provided inspiration and ideas about a topic and a project that others shook their heads over.

1 The sociality of things

Introduction

The hand reaches out for the kettle, lifts it off its stand and places the spout under the tap. Water flows. The kettle is returned to its stand and a movement of the thumb has set it going as the hand leaves the handle, the flow of electricity indicated by a warm red light. The water soon boils and, with a click, the kettle turns itself off. The hand lifts the kettle to pour the boiling water into a cup with a teabag in it. This action is a routine sequence that many people do many times a day, more or less without thinking. It is not easy to do with one's eyes shut – although the 'look' of the kettle is familiar, sight helps to co-ordinate the positioning of the hand as it closes on the kettle, and the kettle as it closes on the tap and then as it is returned back to its stand. But the body's familiarity with the kettle means that the hand is oriented to its handle before it gets close; the hand is open enough to easily move into a grip with the thumb opposed to four fingers and it is prepared for the vertical handle of a 'jug' kettle or the horizontal handle of a traditional kettle. The thumb 'knows' where the switch is and whether to press or push to release power.

I've described someone using a plastic jug kettle that plugs directly onto its stand and fills through a filter in the spout. A few years ago the kettle would be much more likely to be made of metal and thus be heavier and its external surface would much more likely be hot; it would have had a plug attaching a lead directly into the kettle which would have stood on feet but with no stand. The kettle would have had to be unplugged first and filled by lifting the lid to let the water enter the body of the kettle; the spout would have been too narrow for filling. Electric power would have been via the plug and the switch would most likely have been at the wall; the user would have had to switch on and then off when the kettle boiled. And a few years before that the kettle might have been made of aluminium and designed for putting on a gas cooker with a large spout for filling and a cap with a whistle. Or we may go back to the turn of the twentieth century when the kettle would have had a handle, a spout and a lid but be designed to hang over a range. Made of much heavier metal, its handle would have been grasped with some sort of cloth and probably using two hands. The range might have had its own water tank built in but water might well have had to be pumped and carried to the kitchen.

The relationship between material objects and human bodies is characteristic of a particular culture – it is precisely this that has enabled archaeologists and anthropologists to study 'exotic' cultures, displaced in place or time, in the absence of a contemporary documentary account of the culture. We might even say that the material stuff of a people provides a document of the culture and, of course, its documents, whether gravestones, pen and ink writing or typescript, are material objects too. What is noticeable in contemporary societies is that the complexity of material culture has increased at an unprecedented speed and this has been connected with a very rapid change in the material culture of modern societies. Researchers have commented on the impact of this change before – here is Michel de Certeau's colleague Luce Giard commenting in 1994 on the change in kitchen equipment from traditional hand tools to the modern battery of specific tools, often electrically powered, often with attachments, tools like the food processor:

> The change involves not only the utensil or tool and the gesture that uses it, but the *instrumentation relationship* that is established between the user and the object used. In the past, the cook used a simple tool, of a primary kind, that also fulfilled simple functions; her hand furnished the kinetic energy, she directed the progress of the operation, supervised the succession of action sequences, and could mentally represent the process for herself. Today, she employs an elaborate tool, of a secondary kind, that requires complicated handling; she truly understands neither its principle nor the way it works. She feeds this technical object with ingredients to be transformed, then unleashes the movement by pushing a button, and collects the transformed matter without having controlled the intervening steps in the operation.
>
> (de Certeau 1998: 211–12)[1]

The change in the way that objects are incorporated into activities such as preparing food is not simply a change in the objects, it is also a change in the embodied practices, the 'gestures' with which the objects are used. But further than that, Giard is commenting on a change in the way that the social actor interacts with the object that transforms their relation to the action and to the process. This is a late modern equivalent in everyday life to the transformation in the work process that Marx described in relation to the mechanization of production in early modernity (see Chapter 2). The change in the 'instrumentation relationship' is there even in the automatic electric kettle where the source of power is virtually invisible and its connection with the kettle almost incidental, and where its control is ceded to the object. The user does not see the element, does not confront the connection to the power and probably does not know where or precisely how the kettle 'knows' when to switch off. As Giard acknowledges, the material transformation of the domestic kitchen does save time and effort, increases comfort and hygiene but at the cost of 'the ancient balances in the transmission of savoir faire and the management of time' (de Certeau 1998: 212). What de Certeau and his colleagues call 'practices', that is, an embodied sequence of habitual or repeated actions that incorporate 'savoir faire' or 'know-how', are aspects of material existence learnt through the culture. In Chapter 5 we will see how this cultural knowledge is embedded in routine and repeated actions to become what phenomenologists call 'operational intentionality'.

The materiality of society is usually engaged with on an individual basis because it is the meeting of body and object that constitutes the relationship. Some material objects, buildings, for example, interact with many individuals at once, but much of the material environment that constitutes the culture of a society is interacted with by individuals one at a time. Not only the kettle and kitchen equipment but the furniture we use and the tools for everyday living (pens, pencils, mobile phones, personal computers, cars, clothes, and so on) are interacted with on an individual basis. It is even as individuals that we interact with buildings simultaneously, our minded bodies negotiating our own route at our pace, for our purposes. Groups of people do react together but most often to a performed cultural event (a theatrical performance, a public speech or a football match) rather than as an interaction with a material object. So it is through the direct interaction between individuals and material objects that the culture is mediated: the objects have embedded within the materiality of their design and manufacture a series of cultural values that shape the practices, both of body and of mind, by which those objects are used. Of course, on the other end of these material interactions are other people who are both shaping and sharing the culture: those who design and make the artefacts we live with and those who benefit from our material interactions, such as the friend for whom the tea is made.

Studying humans and things

The issue of interaction between human beings and their material environment has long been a concern within anthropology as the study of human beings in all their cultural variation. Anthropology often focuses on particular cultures but underlying such study is a concern with what makes the life of human beings possible; what is characteristic of human being as distinct from any other animal species. In studying distinct cultures, the material life of a people is inseparable from the religion, rituals or customs of their cultural existence and sometimes it has provided a particular focus for making sense of a particular culture. Malinowski's (1922) interest in the Trobriand Islanders' exchange of shells in the Kula ring, and the building of sea-going canoes to transport them, is one of the most famous examples in the anthropological literature that led to decades of discussion and re-analysis (see e.g. Miller 1987: 60–1). Among the commentators was Marcel Mauss who exerted considerable influence over the development of anthropological understanding of material culture with his discussion of the gift – in which a certain measure of human agency is invested in objects that are passed between human beings according to a set of cultural codes: 'Things possess a personality, and the personalities are in some way the permanent things of the clan. Titles, talismans, copper objects and the spirits of the chiefs are both homonyms and synonyms of the same nature and performing the same function' (1990: 46). Objects that are given create obligations of reciprocity as well as symbolizing social status. This strand of cultural anthropology has laid considerable emphasis on the capacity of material objects to sustain social relationships and manage a cultural order – it has given rise to an anthropological interest in 'consumption' as the commodified equivalent of this process within modern, capitalist societies (Veblen 1925; Douglas and Isherwood 1979; Miller 1987; McCracken 1988;).

The emphasis in the anthropological interest in consumption has been in the capacity for material objects to symbolize or represent social relationships but Marcel Mauss's anthropology has also given rise to a different tradition in which more attention is paid to the embodied relationship with material objects. In 1934 Mauss delivered a lecture on the 'Techniques of the Body' (1973) pointing out that how people moved their bodies was not simply 'natural', or animalistic, but was in some senses 'cultural'. Mauss discusses a number of such techniques including swimming, walking, running and sitting still which were all 'arts of using the human body' that he suggested could be understood in terms of a *habitus*, that is, the 'acquired abilities' that varied 'between societies, educations, proprieties and fashions, prestiges' (1973: 73). What interested him was that this cultural variation was not an abstract or purely mental capacity but was a blend of biological, sociological and psychological features that were acquired by members of society through imitation and through action. The techniques of the body were not created by a cognitive grasping of concepts and ideas but were generated and transmitted through the work of collective and individual practical reason. Mauss clarifies what he means by a technique as an action of the body that is 'effective' and 'traditional' and is realized and experienced as 'actions of a mechanical, physical or physio-chemical order' that treat the body as an instrument (1973: 75). Now Mauss was principally concerned with ways of moving and placing the body in its environment, what we might call bodily hexis (Bourdieu 1990: 69–70), but one example he gave involving haptics (the sense of touch) was of soldiers during the First World War digging trenches. He describes how French soldiers could not use English spades and English soldiers could not use French spades, so that each time a division of troops from one country relieved those of another, 8000 spades had to be brought into the battlefield and another 8000 removed. There was a 'manual knack' that took time to learn and was characteristic of the particular culture but here the 'technique' was linked to the particular material form of the spade.

For Mauss, it was the cultural specificity of the bodily technique of digging that was important but recently his ideas have been extended by modern French anthropologists and social scientists. Pierre Parlebas develops Mauss's innovative ideas to suggest that the techniques of the body extend to include the world of material objects and that individual innovation in bodily technique and use of objects is a distinctive feature of action:

> Techniques of the body incorporate material objects. A tennis racket, the wheels of a bicycle, the prow of a boat or the tips of skis will extend the body and become its sensors … Material objects are the recipients of bodily practice.
>
> (1999: 37)[2]

For Parlebas, both bodily techniques and material equipment are embedded in a culture that shapes action in ways that are not easy to recognize from within the situation. A similar approach is explored by Jean-Pierre Warnier (2001) who resists reducing material objects and bodily techniques to a social logic in which simple membership of a culture determines how one relates to objects. He argues that the embodied practices of material culture need to be addressed to understand how human practices are engaged with specific objects to generate different subjectivities within the culture. For Warnier, the subject of social action is not simply a person, but a subject constituted out of material and cultural relations. One of the examples he gives is the child soldier who 'incorporates in his sensori-motricity the kalachnikov and the 4×4 Toyota, plus all the trappings of armed material equipment' and who will at some point be 'fused with his material culture' (2001: 21). Warnier's powerful argument is that while these various pieces of equipment may be read as signs, it is through their daily use for months on end that they become part and parcel of the child's subjectivity that transforms his relationship with other selves. We cannot begin to understand the practices of killing and maiming without recognizing the complexity of this compound subjectivity in which the social actor includes both equipment and embodied practices. Drawing on the work of the psychoanalyst Serge Tisseron (1999), Warnier is keen to introduce the emotional relationship between the individual and the object by which the social and cultural significance of things is sustained. But reading signs and analysing discourses are insufficient to understand material practices and Warnier and his colleagues (see e.g. Warnier and Julien 1999) propose that what is needed is a 'praxeology', by which they mean a science of motricity that can be used to develop an analysis of sensori-affectivo-motor culture. The attempt to understand the lived relationship between humans and objects that constitutes the social, alongside the complexity of discursive and emotional relationships between humans, is the concern of this book. However, the emphasis in Warnier's praxeology is on the way that subjectivity is enhanced as material forms extend the possible actions of the human body; it is the subjectivizing of objects that he and his colleagues focus on, rather than the interaction between subjects and objects. In Chapter 4 I will discuss a number of perspectives on human agency and objects but will argue that human beings interact with objects as well as forming assemblages with them to act in the world. Materiality constitutes an environment for human being with which individual human subjects engage; sometimes materiality remains environment, sometimes it is interacted with directly as distinct objects and sometimes material objects are taken up as tools that extend human instrumentality.

Michael Schiffer is an anthropologist who has recently argued for the importance of studying the interaction between humans and objects because '*human life consists of ceaseless and varied interactions among people and myriad kinds of things*' (1999: 2). Schiffer develops what he calls an ontology to try to make sense of the 'material medium' that human beings are immersed in but he does so from the premise that '*all human behaviour is communication*' (1999: 4). As his argument develops, a new jargon emerges to describe this mode of communicative behaviour that is between human beings but which involves artefacts. Schiffer argues for the importance of artefacts in interpersonal communication, pointing out how clothes, make-up and other forms of adornment, modify the nature of inter-human communication as does the material environment. Again the emphasis is on how materiality extends the performance possibilities of human beings which in turn affects their behaviour. What is rather less credible is that Schiffer does not explain just what the effect is; his general claim that artefacts modify behaviour and interactive performance is well made but we remain unclear what the consequence for communication is. For example, as he describes the various ways body odours are modified through perfumes, soaps as well as tobacco use and foods such as garlic, he argues merely that they affect interaction but does not discuss what the effect on meaning is. It is of course an empirical question and his book is establishing a theoretical position but the general problem remains that the impact of materiality on interaction may often be slight and the relative significance of materiality as opposed to speech and gesture in communicating meaning is not tackled. Schiffer's approach of equating material interaction with communication leads to a limited ontology that, for example, does not allow for the interaction between humans and artefacts to be shaped or oriented for purposes other than communication. Quite simply, much human/object interaction is concerned with work and is not primarily about communication. Whether it is cleaning the house or replacing an exhaust pipe, human interaction with objects is often directed primarily at the material life of humans – sustaining and maintaining artefacts and an environment that enables that particular lifestyle to continue. Schiffer's notion of communication is limited to the transfer of information ('the passage of consequential information from interactor to interactor', 1999: 68) and does not take account of the possibility that interaction between human beings or between human beings and objects can be oriented to emotion (see Tisseron 1999; Chapter 4 below), or pleasure seeking and sensation (see Dant 1999, Howes 2003; Chapter 6 below). Schiffer does theorize the process of interaction between person and object when no other person is involved but always treats it as a form of communication as if information were food enough for the maintenance of bodily and social existence.

Rather than attempt to build an ontology from scratch as Schiffer does, I will work from the ontological discussions of Heidegger and Merleau-Ponty who provide an account of embodied being-in-the-world and its relation with other beings, including those that are non-human. Schiffer does argue persuasively for the potency of material interactions as a vehicle for culture to be exchanged and some of his conceptual apparatus is interesting. For example, he takes up the idea of 'registration' to refer to the way that the human sensory apparatus responds to the world around it. Rather than the common-sense term 'attention', the concept of registration does not suggest wakefulness or particular conscious activity: 'registration may be conscious or nonconscious, explicit or implicit, and voluntary or involuntary' (Schiffer 1999: 105). This concept allows for considerable variation in the way that a body apprehends the material world during interaction with it and the way that this is managed within the being, a process Schiffer calls 'weighting'. In some of his modes of material interaction, Schiffer allows for direct interaction between a person and an object in which the weighting of registration varies between the object, a tool and the environment as the interaction proceeds. For example, he writes of someone carving a duck on his front porch; as the interaction proceeds, the information received through the actions of carving are weighted and will affect

the next stroke of the knife. Information from the environment is simultaneously registered but differently weighted – although someone coming
along will be registered and may be weighted sufficiently to yield a response
such as a greeting (Schiffer 1999: 107–8). A further contribution from
anthropology about agency, Alfred Gell's discussion of art as agency, will be
discussed in Chapter 4.

Schiffer's close attention to the process of interaction and the gleaning
of information from a range of material entities is most interesting and is,
sadly, not matched by the discussions of materiality and society within the
sociological literature. In the sociology of science and technology there
have been a number of discussions on sociality and materiality (Law and
Mol 1995; Knorr-Cetina 1997 – see Brenna et al. 1998; Preda 1999; Dant
and Martin 2001; Pels, et al. 2002; Bruun and Langlais 2003; Thurk and Fine
2003). Much of this material has drawn on the stimulation of Latour,
Callon and Akrich's 'actor-network theory' which will receive some attention in Chapter 4. In general, these commentaries attempt to grasp the
nature of materiality as a form that can be related to society at an abstract
or theoretical level. This continues a debate about the general relationship
between society and technology that will be addressed in Chapter 3. But in
the sociological literature there is little attempt to grasp how social relationships with material objects are formed by attending to the detail of how
contact between social actors and things is achieved. An exception is the
work of Christian Heath and his colleagues who have developed a distinctive approach to the study of workplaces (see Heath et al. 2000; Luff et al.
2000). They have gathered and analysed video data in a variety of settings
where material objects are part of the activity of work and have attended to
some of the details of the interaction between humans and objects.[3] Their
focus of attention has primarily been on how material objects become
incorporated into interaction between humans and how attention to material objects is inserted into exchanges of talk. This body of work brings
together some of the rigour of conversational analysis and the attention to
embodied, non-verbal communication that was a feature of Heath's work
on medical encounters (1986). This style of research brings fine detail to
understanding how collaborative work is achieved through convergence of
action, co-participation in decisions and the sharing of judgements and
assessments of situations. What their studies show is how objects are incorporated into collaborative work because the work arises from information
received from or about objects (and is often directed to manipulating
objects) and because objects – such as telephones and computer screens – are
tools for mediating between co-workers. Inspired by this fascinating work, I
have taken a different direction to focus on the direct interaction between
human beings and objects without being necessarily concerned about interaction with co-participants. This is because the cultural significance of the

interaction is often between those who are not co-present: those who made the object and its end user. It is the detailed nature of how this interaction is undertaken that is the focus of this book and the approach of the book is to explore a series of discourses that potentially address the relationship between society and materiality.

Material interaction

A running example, though not the only one, that will be used during the book is the nature of interaction with cars. The motor car emerged into and participated in the development of capitalist production early in the twentieth century to become a key component in modern and late modern culture (see Chinoy 1955; Goldthorpe et al. 1968; Beynon 1973; Altshuler et al. 1984; Sachs 1992; Gartman 1994; O'Connell 1998; Thoms et al. 1998; Adams 1999; Hawkin et al. 1999; Urry 1999, 2000; Miller 2001b). The trajectory of the car was very much linked to the development of the mass production of objects but by the middle of the twentieth century became significant in the development of late modern modes of consumption, lifestyle and the organization of societies. The car as an object that shapes much of social life at the beginning of the twenty-first century is only just beginning to be recognized. As John Urry puts it: 'The car's significance is that it reconfigures civil society involving distinct ways of dwelling, travelling and socialising in, and through, an automobilized time-space. Civil societies of the west are societies of automobility'.(2000: 59). The car is at once a social object and at the same time one that is largely interacted with by an individual, the driver (Dant 2000a; Dant and Martin 2001; Dant 2004). As well as an object that is produced and consumed, the car also has to be maintained if its owner is to be able to continue to participate in modern society and the repair and maintenance of the car offer an opportunity to study interaction with objects close up. This type of work is routine and everyday to those who do it and yet, unlike the filling of the kettle, is somewhat exotic to those of us who do not. Interaction between human and object during the repair and maintenance of cars is relatively easy to observe because of the size of the objects involved and the pace at which work proceeds. Although it involves many modern electronic and sophisticated pieces of equipment, the wielding of handtools, particularly the spanner, is the principal means of working on the car and its components. Chapter 6 will focus on embodied material interaction and draw on illustrative examples from video data collected during an ESRC-funded research project undertaken at the University of East Anglia.[4]

Overview of the book

In this introduction I have mentioned all the chapters that follow but I will briefly summarize here what their themes are. Each chapter addresses a discourse or group of discourses that in some way bear on the topic of materiality and society. There is a structure of moving progressively from society as history towards the micro-level of interaction between a person and an object – the argument of this book is that ultimately this is how material culture is mediated in its embodied, non-symbolic mode. In Chapter 2 I will discuss Braudel's idea of 'material civilization' as a way of understanding the emergence of modernity as a transformation in the relationship between society and materiality. Here I will also briefly discuss the importance of material relations in the emergence of the capitalist mode of production that Marx describes as well as the place of materiality in the attempt to understand consumption in modern societies. The emphasis of studies of consumption has been on the 'meanings' or significance of social status of objects but that has overlooked the lived and practical relations with things. As modernity has developed, the possibility that things may come to dominate society has been a theme for social theories about technology and this will be addressed in Chapter 3. In anthropology, psychology and sociology there are various views of objects that attribute them some degree of social 'agency' which is the topic of Chapter 4. These views treat materiality as disaggregated into things, usually things embedded in human or social relations, rather than as a collective whole such as 'technology'. In Chapter 5 I will explore some of the features of being-in-the-world through the phenomenology of Heidegger and Merleau-Ponty as tackling rather more fundamentally the possibility of human relations with things. Chapter 6 will develop this approach and apply it to the process of ordinary material interaction – specifically between technicians, their tools and the cars they are working on. In Chapter 7 I will make some concluding remarks about how the relations between materiality and society are changing in the late modern societies of the twenty-first century.

2   Material civilization

Introduction

Sociology has not traditionally concerned itself with the material stuff of life much. Its principal concern has been with how human beings live together and, as a collectivity, create an entity with a form that cannot be reduced to the life of individuals or the biological propensity of humans as animals to survive – society. It is the connections between humans, that are interactive, communicative and emotional, that create the institutions and patterns of social relationship characteristic of the form of society. That form is more complex than can be accounted for simply in terms of instinct or genetic inheritance so that the study of societies is distinct from biology or zoology. Perhaps the most significant feature of human societies that distinguishes them from the social groups of other species is symbolic language that is transmitted through vocalization and inscribed into representational images and writing. But symbolic communication is not separate as a distinctive faculty of biological human being because it emerges as part and parcel of social patterns of action and behaviour, that include family arrangements, religion, legal systems and economic arrangements. There is a contiguity between sociology and a series of other disciplines that study various aspects of human collective existence, particularly history, anthropology, economics, politics, philosophy and psychology, each of which focus on a different aspect or area of human collective behaviour.

It is often difficult to distinguish sociology from these various disciplines, to mark what is distinctly sociological about a perspective, a theory or a line of argument that could not be incorporated within these other disciplines. If there is a distinction, then it appears to have two characteristics. First, the sociological perspective suggests that there is something about the way that humans form into collective groups that is imperative for any individual's specific action within the group. This is not to suggest that society is determinative of individual or even collective action, merely that the responses of other members of the group to an individual's actions in a social context can be more or less anticipated. Second, sociology is largely concerned with the form of *modern* societies, with those that have emerged after a transformatory period of industrialization. It would be strange to suggest that there were no 'societies' prior to industrialization but the distinctive discipline of sociology emerged in the attempt to grasp the effects of industrialization. The form of pre-modern societies has been of interest to historians, anthropologists and archaeologists who have studied societies of the past but sociologists have studied such societies principally in order to understand the transition to modern societies. The effects of industrialization are largely to do with new economic, political and legal arrangements that emerged during a period of rapid transformation over a couple of centuries in the way people worked and lived in industrialized societies. The form that societies take, and that sociology is interested in, has sometimes been concerned with social structure – the ways in which individuals are situated within sub-groups or strata within the society – and at other times has been more concerned with social agency – the ways in which individuals realize themselves within the context of social constraints. These dimensions of structure and agency, of group formation and individual response, have led to the development of theories and methods that emphasize one or the other, but sociology is always concerned to specify what constitutes society and how it bears on the actions of individuals. The transition to modernity has brought with it changes in social structure and in the relationship between individuals and their society that sociology has attempted to understand.

For reasons that are tied up with the historical process of institutionalized knowledge, sociology has not, on the whole, been concerned with the material life of human beings. This is strange because one of the most dramatic impacts of industrialization has been on the transformation of human material life. The ways of meeting material needs for sustenance, shelter, comfort, body maintenance, mobility and aesthetic pleasure have been transformed in modernity. The changes have perhaps been of less significance for the wealthy few who have always been able to ensure that they have sufficient in the way of material goods (in terms of food, comfort, adornment and decoration), even at the expense of those such as slaves or serfs who lived an impoverished material life. Modern industrial societies remain strikingly unequal in the material quality of life of their members, but there has been nonetheless, for the great majority, a dramatic transformation in their material life as compared with even a couple of decades ago. Material standards are better in the twenty-first century for most people in the rich industrialized countries than they were for even the rich few of the eighteenth century. Of course, this does not mean that people are happier or any more fulfilled, it does not even mean that they have more autonomy over their lives – but it does mean that they have more material opportunities to live in comfort, to travel, to be healthy, to eat sufficiently and to enjoy aesthetic pleasures of the senses.

Classical sociology, which emerged to account for and explain the social consequences of modernity, set the agenda for the discipline for the last century. Even today students are taught the writings of these founders who established what the proper concerns of sociology are – and rightly so, since their work has a bearing on the sociologies that have emerged since, whether it is functionalism, postmodernism, critical realism or feminism. The classic sociology of Marx, Weber, Durkheim and Simmel give us some basic conceptual tools with which to understand the transition from what we might call 'traditional' society to 'modern' – industrialized, capitalist, urbanized – society. Sociology as a distinct discipline emerges to understand precisely this new form of society, to grasp its new economic and social order and analyse how it is different from what has gone before. In this chapter I will explore some of the ways in which sociology has engaged with, touched upon or avoided the process that Braudel calls 'material civilization' – the impact of material life on the changing form of society.

Marx: a materialist sociology

It is Marx whose analysis of the economic transformation to a capitalist mode of production identifies changes in social relations of great signifi-cance, most importantly the emergence of a new class order based on rela-tionship to the means of production. The class distinctions between the bourgeoisie and the proletariat are the social concomitants of economic changes such as the division of labour and a reorganization of work around the commodity, the factory and the city. These themes become key areas of debate for classical sociology that continued well into the latter half of the twentieth century, but Marx and Engels's analysis of the mode of produc-tion followed a distinctly materialist understanding of history. Engels's materialism made a link between the scientific understanding of society and the scientific understanding of the material world – mathematical mechanics, the physics of electricity and biology. Physical science had demonstrated that knowledge, practical knowledge, was needed to address the material substance of the world empirically and resist distraction by ideas, fantasies and myths. In *Anti-Dühring* (1936) and the *Dialectics of Nature* (1940), he attempts to chase out the remains of metaphysical thought from the natural, material sciences and to identify universal or transcendent laws that will persist across all scientific knowledge. Engels demonstrates an obsessive concern with dialectics as a mode of thought based on a 'natural' process – something is true because it is evident in the material world – that begins to sound like the very transcendent, meta-physical law he wishes to dispel.[1] But Marx's materialism is more subtle and is more concerned with the workings of political economy than with establishing a scientific method of dialectics that will span the study of history and that of physics, chemistry and biology. The young Marx accuses Hegel of the 'crassest materialism' when he treats human status differences and property rights as the same thing – Marx wittily suggests that it appears as if it is the land that inherits the property owner, since it is only the land that endures (Marx 1975: 174–5). Marx's own materialism is based on recognizing the distinction between politics – which attributes social status – and the material world which includes both the life of humans and the land upon which they work. This analysis also drives his critique of Feuerbach's materialism whom he accused of focusing on 'abstract thinking' and 'contemplation' instead of 'practical, human-sensuous activity' – material human action (Marx 1975: 422). Following Feuerbach, Marx and Engels set out the basis of their materialism as lying in production, through which individuals produce their 'mode of life' – not just the physical and material aspects but all aspects – while at the same time their nature depends on the material conditions determining production.[2]

It is, however, in Volume 1 of *Capital* (1976) that Marx draws on the material world of lived sensuous experience to explain the mechanics of the capitalist mode of production. He describes the effects of work on the lives and bodies of the working class (Marx 1976: Chapter 10, 'The Working Day') which together with Engels's (1845) account of the conditions of the working class are key documents in the changing material civilization of modernity. In later chapters Marx (1976: Chapters 14 and 15) discusses the impact of machinery on the industrialized division of labour in manufacture as it emerged from its evolution over the previous two centuries from traditional handicrafts. Unlike Durkheim and Weber, when discussing the division of labour, Marx explores the material effect on a worker of the continuous repetition of the same simple operation over a whole life which 'converts his body into the automatic, one-sided implement of that operation' (1976: 458). He recognizes that it leads to an increased specialization of tools as well as of the worker to produce a distinctive material culture of production that reduces the total amount of labour power required for the finished object but at the same time alters the worker's relationship with his tools and with the object itself. An efficient division of labour requires that workers are brought together to live in a greater density than would be necessary for handicraft production and, as Marx spells out, this interaction affects social organization beyond work. Both geographical communities and the communities of production or 'guilds' are social patterns linked to the traditional organization of production. But it is the distinctively capitalist organization of a division of labour within one workshop or factory in which all contribute to the production of a final commodity while none own the means of production, that brings about the particular material form of life of the proletariat that 'attacks the individual at the very roots of his life' (1976: 484). The material civilization of individual workers suffers as they become subjected to the requirements of capitalist production and community identity is displaced by their commodified relationship with the capitalist and the factory.

Machinery transforms the material life of the worker, not simply by the replacement of him or her as a source of power, but by taking over and linking together tools to replace a series of workers (Marx 1976: 494–5). Mechanized tools can become much larger and more powerful than could be handled by even groups of workers and they prompt further mechanization within an industry or factory. Industrial machinery, as well as providing motive force, takes over the worker's skills in manipulating tools and dictates the pace, force and placement of action and so the worker has to 'adapt his own movements to the uniform and unceasing motion of an automaton' (Marx 1976: 546). The factory itself becomes an extended form of the machine in which the worker's freedom, both physical and mental, is constrained and directed according to the requirements of the machine.[3] Beyond the factory, machine production also changed human relations as women and children were employed to replace male labourers – at a lower rate of pay, of course. As Marx puts it, 'Previously the worker sold his own labour-power, which he disposed of as a free agent, formally speaking. Now he sells wife and child. He has become a slave-dealer' (1976: 519). The working day is also lengthened because the machinery is a capital investment that can operate independently of the rhythms of day or season.

The machines do have a material life of their own, which again Marx spells out; they deteriorate both through wear in use and through the ageing or degradation of material over time, whether used or not (1976: 528). But the material life of machines means that they are best used intensively so their attendant workers were also to be used intensively by speeding up the machines, despite the greater exhaustion and risk of injury. The workers of the industrializing world did not accept these changes in their material life without complaint and resistance and again Marx carefully documents these struggles (1976: 553–64). The resistance of workers through strikes provided further encouragement for the capitalist to introduce machines to replace them, especially with 'self-acting' tools. If the price was right, most workers could be replaced by automatic machinery and those workers who remained were easily replaced by other workers because skill was embedded in machines rather than in workers. The increase in productivity stimulated all sorts of other economic activity, most importantly it stimulated consumer demand – as the material conditions of the factory workers declined, the material possibilities for the extending middle classes increased.[4] As wealth was created within a locality, there was an increased demand and possibility for public works (canals, docks, bridges, tunnels, etc.) and ancillary industries (Marx mentions gas-works, telegraphy, photography, steam navigation and railways, 1976: 573). Laying-off workers as they were replaced by machines also created cheap domestic labour and led to an increase in 'the number of modern domestic slaves' (Marx 1976: 575).

Marx pays close attention to the changing material culture of produc-tion, based on the reports of factory inspectors, children's employment commissions, public health reports and so on, to provide a detailed account of the material process of alienation that he had earlier discussed in the abstract in his *Economic and Philosophical Manuscripts* (1975: 322–34). He may stand out among classical social theorists for his detailed account of material civilization as regards production, but he has hardly anything to say about the changes in everyday material life that came with industri-alization. Despite his distinction between 'use' and 'exchange' value that is central to his account of the commodity form in *Capital*, Marx does not discuss use-value and how it is realized in material life. The distinction is a technical one which enables him to analyse the economic relations of exchange-value independently of the ways in which goods affect the routine activities of everyday life. For Marx, use-value 'has no existence apart from' its physical properties whereas exchange-value is a 'form of appearance' since it is an abstract relational value, independent of use and 'therefore does not contain an atom of use-value' (1976: 127–8). But this analysis treats use-value as a constant quality of the object and disconnects it from the ways in which goods are used. Use-values are not discrete, con-stituting a single function for a single material form because any given object may have more than one use (a bucket may be for putting slops in, for getting water or for turning upside down to sit or stand on). Use-values will vary according to social circumstances (buckets for carrying water have extra value when the water is cut off and it has to be carried from a stand-pipe) and these varying circumstances of use will interact with exchange-values. In other words, there is more than an atom of use-value in exchange-value and use-value has a social dimension that spills over into exchange in a complex series of ways.

These problems with Marx's theory of use- and exchange-value have been commented on before many times and in much greater detail (e.g. Baudrillard [1972] 1981; Sahlins 1976). Baudrillard argued that use-value and utility itself became a 'fetishised social relation' in Marx's writing because it was based on an abstraction of a system of needs (Baudrillard 1981: 131). His solution was to add a third dimension of 'sign-value' to the commodity to account for the cultural processes that connect use- and exchange-values. Use-values are negotiated in a social context and while in modern society we may readily point to the role of advertising and sign exchange in prompting us to recognize new use-values, it must be the case in *any* human society that imitation is one of the ways that use-values are recognized and taken up. A new form of plough or water fountain is its own advertisement that will attract interest and replication if it demonstrates a use. Marx asserts that the exchange-value of commodities is 'totally independent of their use-value' (1976: 128) on the grounds that while use-values are qualities in things, exchange-values are merely to do with quantity. He argues that commodities are 'merely congealed quantities of homogenous human labour' (Marx 1976: 128) but this is because, for theoretical purposes, he has abstracted the commodity form from use so that 'It is no longer a table, a house, a piece of yarn or any other useful thing. All its sensuous characteristics are extinguished' (Marx 1976: 128).

Marx seems to recognize a more complex relationship between consumption and production in a famous section in the *Grundrisse* (1973) where he says 'consumption mediates production, in that it alone creates for the products the subject for whom they are products ... a garment becomes a real garment only in the act of being worn; a house where no one lives is in fact not a real house; thus the product, unlike a mere natural object, proves itself to be, *becomes*, a product only through consumption' (1973: 91). This recognition of the continuity between the work of production and the use of consumption suggests that exchange is based on more than relative quantities of commodities. Later in this passage Marx discusses consumption as the 'motive' for production that suggests 'an internal image, as a need, as drive and as purpose' (1973: 91–2). Consumption as a form of production and the role of art in responding to production are alluded to, suggesting that both use and beauty are social products.[5] However, these brief notes by Marx stand alone and apart from his substantive discussions which address political economy.[6] In *Capital* (1976) Marx explains at length the operation of money as capital and the manipulation of the labour market to extract surplus value, but he defines the material needs of a worker for social reproduction as an average (Marx 1976: 129). The complexity of use-values in the lives of workers and the significance of consumption in the relations of capitalism are never tackled.

The strangeness of Marx's distinction between use-value and exchange-value is linked to the investment of labour power in the object. What Marx does not explore are the variations between commodities and their varying capacity to meet material needs and the variations in the material relations by which commodities are produced and, with a few exceptions such as Baudrillard and Sahlins, there has been no substantial rethinking of the nature of use-value.[7] It is the way that something is taken up in the various material activities of humans that determines its use-value and will have an impact on its exchange-value. As material civilization develops, so will use- and exchange-values – they are not simply determined by the quantity of labour power congealed in them. Although Marx brings a materialist perspective to understanding how modern society has been transformed in terms of production, his analysis does not provide a sufficient basis for a sociological grasp of the material civilization of modernity.

Simmel: value and money

Classical social theory can be seen as a response to Marx's analysis of the process of change that brought modern societies into being. Among the classical theorists, Simmel responds to the political economic analysis of modernity with a sociology of 'forms' and of the transformation of 'socia-tion' in modernity that were consequent on changes in the material life of modernity (Simmel 1950). The sociological 'physiognomies' that he explores (the stranger, the metropolitan, the adventurer, the miser, and so on) emerge in the context of the material bustle of the modern city and the practical changes in the lives of people that produced new types of social relations (Simmel 1971a). In distinction from Marx, he argues from a phe-nomenological position that cultural value originates in subjective desire for the object that lies outside the individual; the object is, he says, a product of consciousness and may of course be another person or have an abstract form (Simmel 1990: 66). The object formed by desire may, however, be material – a thing, a good or a commodity – and it is through subjective enjoyment or consumption that the value of the object is effaced.

Aesthetic value in the object is somewhat different and depends on maintaining a distance in which the subject recognizes some autonomous significance inherent in the object; pleasure is derived not from direct con-sumption but by contemplation, by reserve and remoteness (Simmel 1990: 73). Now it is in the exchange of objects that social subjects exchange values and value becomes an objective characteristic of the culture of their society. For Simmel, exchange is the purest form of interaction between social subjects, and in the case of material exchange involves sacrifice, for-going the usefulness of the good that is exchanged (1990: 82). This is an account of the exchange-value and money system that is grounded in a very different orientation to material existence than that of Marx. Where Marx sees the work of production, Simmel sees the pleasure of consump-tion. Whereas Marx sees exchange-value as a product of capitalist social relations, Simmel sees it as a fundamental social relation with a direct sub-jective cost. Whereas Marx sees money as a symbolic erasure of the true value of goods in the labour that went into their production, Simmel sees money as the symbolic representation of the objective cultural determina-tion of value in goods.

Simmel's perspective that the basis of culture lies in the exchange of value, means that he is sensitive to the impact of cultural shifts in the material life of a society. He responds to the impact of changing modes of transport, street lighting, domestic technology and to the importance of outward appearance, adornment and fashion. Whereas Marx emphasized the impact of modern production techniques on the workers and the economy of production, Simmel commented on how they changed material relations within societies to give their general social life a modern quality. The sheer volume of objects, their increasing autonomy and their specialization changed the relationship between social subject and the object, reducing the personal involvement with them and increasing social distance. As Simmel put it: 'Objects and people have become separated from one another' (1990: 460). His account of money recognizes that its materiality can substitute for the complexity of social relations needed to engage in the assessment and negotiation of value. If the process is autonomized, as it is with the slot machine, the direct human interaction of exchange is substituted altogether.

Just as money interposed itself in human interactions, so new technologies interposed themselves in subjective relationships with the material world itself to produce 'a freedom from direct concern with things and from a direct relationship with them' (Simmel 1990: 469). The example he gives is the typewriter which reduces the individual and subjective form of handwriting to mechanical uniformity and, in removing the most personal element, allows the individual to guard their subjective spirituality. Simmel recognized the cultural significance of technology and its predominance in shaping the style of life in modernity with the consequence that the social subject became more individualized and more able to turn in on her or himself by substituting relationships with material objects for social relationships. He regretted the impact on the spiritual and inner life of modern human beings and pointed out that, as against the enthusiasm for electric lighting, 'the essential thing is not the lighting itself but what becomes more fully visible,' and, as against the speed of communication enabled by the telephone and telegraph, 'what really matters is the value of what one has to say' (Simmel 1990: 482). Rather than seeing modernity as a period of the social mass, he saw its significance and intellectual potential as located in the form of objects and machines; he warned not of the revolt of the masses against their slavery but 'the revolt of objects' against theirs (Simmel 1990: 483).

Unlike Durkheim's discussion of the increase in physical density within modernity as having directly moral effects, Simmel recognizes that the increasing density of population in metropolitan cities leads to physiological and mental effects that in turn create a 'blasé' attitude, not only towards people but also towards things. The close proximity of many people to each other required developing a disinterest in their lives and their individuality, a reserve that would treat them as more akin to objects than to social subjects. The close proximity to things of increasing variety and complexity is managed by dealing with them through the intermediary of money which 'hollows out the core of things, their peculiarities, their specific values, and their uniqueness and incomparability in a way that is beyond repair' (Simmel 1971a: 330). Simmel's sociological interest was, however, in the new forms of sociation, especially those exclusively concerned with sociability, that emerge in modernity to substitute for the increasingly mechanical social relations surrounding economic interaction. One of the reasons why his remarkable essay on fashion does not date is precisely because he does not discuss fashions at all – he does not discuss the lived relations with clothes, only the cultural dynamics of imitation and differentiation that fashion realizes (Simmel 1971b).

Traditional social theory

Marx is alone among the classical sociologists in claiming to be a 'materialist' and addressing the material life of people and while Simmel takes a contrasting perspective on what shapes modern societies, Marx develops an analysis of social forms rather than pursue their material dimension. What the other, later, classical sociologists do is to respond to some of the themes raised by Marx and tease out the significance of the social transformations of modernity, often distinguishing the social from the economic. Durkheim's *The Division of Labour* (1933) is a prime example of this; he says hardly anything about the division of labour as such, treating its material form as understood, and discusses instead 'social solidarity' and the 'conscience collective'. There is no attempt to understand what labour is or even how the practices of labour are changed by its increasing division. Durkheim says: 'Things, to be sure, form part of society just as much as persons, and they play a specific role in it … We may say that there is a solidarity of things whose nature is quite special and translates itself outside through judicial consequences of a very particular character' (1993: 115). However, it is only the juridical nature of property law and its relation to mechanical solidarity that he goes on to discuss while any other role for 'things' in social solidarity is left aside. Further on in *The Division of Labour*, Durkheim does recognize that the shift to modernity is linked to the changing material needs and pleasures of workers so that 'individuals really feel the need of more abundant products or products of a better quality' (1933: 272). But, bizarrely, he explains this in terms of the 'more voluminous and delicate brain' of the industrial worker which 'makes greater demands than a less refined one' (Durkheim 1933: 272) such as that of the agricultural worker. The refining of needs for products is not something that Durkheim discusses beyond suggesting that, like sex, once experienced, desire for the pleasures of things becomes established as an everyday need. It is the quintessentially *immaterial* aspects of society that interest him and they need to be grasped by intermediary indicators such as the legal system, itself a cultural process that is treated as primarily of ethical significance.

Weber's (1978) sociology is more oriented to social action than Durkheim's attempts to reduce the abstract qualities of societies to 'facts', but Weber's themes are also persistently immaterial: economic relations, meanings and motivations, power, regulation, law, authority, religion, the city, music and, above all, rationality. It is the development of a mode of thought, instrumental rationality, as it is applied to the relations between men and women that fascinates Weber. But he has very little to say about the relation between that same mode of thought and the material world, even though it is the locus in which, arguably, it first demonstrated its efficacy in the development of machine technology. Weber's analysis of the division of labour, unlike Durkheim's, does recognize the differentiation between trades but his interest is in how people are organized into economic units that have sociological characteristics rather than in what people *do* in any material sense. The utility of goods is the desirable or practical service that they provide but how this is adjudged or lived out is of no interest to Weber. Wants are never specified or discussed but the various social arrangements by which they are met are set out. The variability of need, want and desire, and the tension between aesthetic and functional dimensions are overlooked as Weber explores the mechanisms of the market and the historically emerging logic of economic systems. For Weber, the material trajectory of human lives is always mediated by economic relations and it is these that he discusses.

It is the capacity to plan and act systematically within economic action that provides the model for instrumental rationality (Weber 1978: 63–74). Action is rational for Weber when it is 'determined by expectations as to the behaviour of objects in the environment and other human beings; these expectations are used as "conditions" or "means" for the attainment of the actor's own rationally pursued and calculated ends' (1978: 24). And it is 'consociation through exchange in the market' that is the 'archetype of all rational social action' (Weber 1978: 635). Where Simmel saw the distance between people and between people and objects as an unfortunate consequence of the materiality of modernity, Weber sees the impersonality and matter-of-factness, even the distance of its process from the material exchange of goods, as being the qualities that make the market rational. Surprisingly, Weber does not explore the origins of means–ends rationality in the practical action of working with things or in the technological developments that drive the industrialization and modernization that bring about the economic relations of modernity. He specifies that '[o]vert action is not social if it is oriented solely to the behaviour of inanimate objects' (Weber 1978: 22) thereby ruling out by fiat precisely what this book is about – that interaction with inanimate objects is one of the ways that culture is transmitted. Weber does not countenance the possibility that action in relation to objects is 'meaningful' and that such action could be called social because it 'takes account of the behaviour of others' (1978: 4) – even though the behaviour of another might have specifically contributed to the particular form of the object. His approach to sociology is one that addresses social action as that which happens between social actors and, while this may occur in a material context, it has no bearing on the social meanings involved. The idea that objects in any way mediate social relations, even those of economic production, is just not entertained within Weber's sociology.

Marx provides a quite detailed analysis of a changing material civilization in the sphere of production but has little to say about the changing materiality of use or consumption. Simmel may not analyse the material civilization of production or political economy but he does recognize the impact of material life upon the changing social sensibilities of modern people; he describes the substitution of material relationships for social relationships and some changes in the relations between people and things. However, although there is an awareness of the material context of society that seems to be totally absent in the writing of Durkheim or Weber, even for Simmel it is an occasional theme; his principal sociological interest is in relationships between people that produce affiliations, groups, conflict or sociability. The central themes of these classical sociologists are predominantly 'immaterial' overlooking the significance of material civilization in the creation of society. What is absent from Durkheim, Weber and Simmel is any discussion of the material relations of, for example, work or of the consumption and use of material objects. Nor does their sort of sociology consider the routine, habitual, everyday consequences for ordinary people of what were a dramatic set of changes in material life brought about by industrialization.

Theories of consumption

In Marx and Weber we find a concern with the social formations that arise from the emerging economic arrangements of modernity that have remained a consistent theme in sociology ever since. Simmel stands somewhat apart from Marx and Weber in his interest in the sensibility that individuals bring to interactions which, in turn, produce the cultural sphere. Rather than see money, exchange or social groups as determined by economic processes, he sees them as emergent features of sociation, inextricable from the formation of culture and the play of complex interests that extend beyond the economic. But it is Thorstein Veblen, more an economist than a sociologist, who identifies the social dynamics of taste and discrimination as a driving force in the shaping of modern societies. Veblen's account of conspicuous consumption allows that the external, material form of social life, that which is visible as part of the style of life of social groups, is indicative of social structure and is linked to the dynamic of social change. The economic imperative of 'interests' that for Weber remain hidden within the concept of rationality, for Veblen becomes expressed as emulation: 'With the exception of the instinct of self-preservation, the propensity for emulation is probably the strongest and most alert and persistent of the economic motives proper' (Veblen 1925: 85). In pecuniary societies, wealth, beyond meeting purely physical wants, is expended on conspicuous waste, that is consumption that is visible to others and in its excess serves to demonstrate social standing. Members of society follow a standard of living that is equivalent to those who share their class or community; through habit and convention they feel obliged to be seen as members of a particular stratum. They participate in a material life by consuming goods and services and engaging in social activities that conform to the norms of their social group. The driving force of consumption may be the visible emulation of the standard of the peer group, but Veblen points out that canons of decency and taste are established within the social stratum that extend to goods that are unlikely to be seen such as underclothes, kitchen utensils and functional household apparatus (see, for example, his discussion of spoons, 1925: 94–5). The standard of living extends from habits of consumption to habits of thought, including those that apply to aesthetic standards. Taking possession of that which is beautiful and expensive, whether for adornment, display or merely ownership, is to demonstrate pecuniary status and yet the possession of that which is beautiful but of little monetary value – such as readily available cut flowers – accords negative status. Veblen does address the materiality of consumption whether it is clothes, furnishings, gardens or household equipment. But he sees in it simply a sign of social status. Even, and here his argument begins to turn in on itself, the withdrawal from invidious display and comparison is linked to a new mode of signification as the leisure classes indulge in social reform and doing good, thereby showing their lack of need to work.

For Veblen, it appears that material life is primarily about display and emulation; it is the way which the individual lives out their position within social structure. He has little to say about how the life of the individual is shaped by the material situation in which they act but this is because his writing about pecuniary culture is built upon an understanding of human culture as being motivated by the 'instinct for workmanship'. For Veblen, an instinct is the 'conscious pursuit of an objective end' (1914: 5) that becomes a habituated disposition in a social context and while it is applied through the intellect, nonetheless has a biological basis and is inherited. The instinct for workmanship has as its end the 'ways and means, devices and contrivances of efficiency and economy, proficiency, creative work and technological mastery of facts' that contribute to the life of the individual and sustain the social group (Veblen 1914: 33). Since instinctual propensity is a characteristic of the species, it is slow to change and develop but becomes externalized within the culture through the system of technology by which the material life of the group is maintained. But culture is also the source of a contamination of the instinct through religious or other beliefs or through the impact of institutions that maintain, for example, class distinctions. These cultural forces create contradictory imperatives that stop the instinct for workmanship from being as efficient and masterful as it might otherwise be. Religious beliefs or institutional constraints will cut across the most efficient work practices and inhibit technological development.

Veblen describes the various ways in which different races of human beings applied the instinct of workmanship to create distinctive material cultures that pragmatically made use of accumulated skills to transform the material world around them, particularly through working the land and breeding domestic animals. Cultural systems emerge to control the means by which material wealth is obtained, initially through the power of a sovereign or priestly class. Modern material civilization, however, emerges when control is established not through force but through ownership and rights in property, the system that Veblen calls 'pecuniary culture'. Pecuniary culture is competitive according to price and so the principle of efficiency leads to mechanization and to an increase in the scale of production. But while the machinery is owned by individuals, knowledge of how to use it resides in the community and sometimes in certain groups of workers who do not own the material equipment with which their skills are realized. Somewhat like Marx, though in a far more abstract style, Veblen describes how machines substituted for the human actions of handicraft production; 'They are, as they aim to be, labour saving devices, designed to further the workmanlike efficiency of the men in whose hands they are placed' (1914: 238).

For Veblen, the instinct for workmanship, of human effort intelligently and efficiently used to transform the material world for human ends, underlies the emergence of science and technology and even the logic of accountancy. This 'postulate of contact' – work as effort applied directly by the body to material stuff – has its origins in the instinct for workmanship but becomes transformed in machine industry as 'conceptions of mass, velocity, pressure, stress, vibration, displacement and the like' in which an impersonal form of human action is taken as the model of technology and becomes a habit of thought in modernity (Veblen 1914: 330). What is striking, however, is that despite this detailed account of the development of material civilization, Veblen does not apply the same principle of human interaction with the material world when it comes to consumption. Veblen, like Simmel, is sensitive to the impact of emulation on shaping culture but he has no account of the pleasure taken in the object that has been produced. Just as with Marx and Weber, want, need and use are taken by

Veblen as features of the human condition that are self-explanatory and that do not vary in the way they are realized.

Veblen's lead in describing the emulatory function of consumption, of the desire for material goods as based in the social imperative to mark distinction, has been followed in much later writing on consumption by historians (McKendrick et al.; the contributors to Brewer and Porter 1983; McCracken 1988), and anthropologists (Sahlins 1976; Douglas and Isherwood 1979; Miller 1987). Sociologists such as Campbell (1989), Corrigan (1997), and Slater (1997) have combined this concern with the symbolic nature of the material of consumption with economic and ideological interests. However, the dominant theme has been to explore what and how things *mean*, including what things mean in relation to individual identity, but much more importantly what they mean in relation to group or class identity. The material objects of consumption are treated as signifiers of social class and status, telling us about their owners as individuals who have acquired or inherited wealth and the capacity to read and recognize these signs. What is overlooked is how objects are lived with, how their form leads to certain types of actions and curtails others, or how the presence of the objects within a life affects the bodily experience of those who use them. The tendency within the discussion of consumption has been to reduce material culture to a significatory system and to a focus on practices to do with desiring and acquiring objects to achieve social emulation and display status.

For example, Grant McCracken (1988) is unusual among writers on consumption in focusing not on the ideas or motivations behind consumption or on the practices of acquisition but on the possession of material objects. He develops a theory of 'patina', the small signs of visible wear and tear that accumulate on the surface of objects as they age, in which these material marks are to be understood as an indicator of social status. Whereas Marx treats the ageing of machines as a practical and an economic problem, for McCracken, the ageing of material possessions is merely a sign: 'In Western Societies, this physical property is treated as a symbolic property ... exploited to social purpose ... seized upon to encode a vital and unusual status message ... of suggesting that existing status claims are legitimate' (1988: 32). The patina on inherited silver plate, for example, is a 'kind of proof of the family's longevity and the duration of their gentle status' (McCracken 1988: 32). McCracken theorizes about patina with the help of Lévi-Strauss's structuralism, Veblen's conspicuous consumption and Peirce's concept of the icon and proposes a 'history' of patina that eventually gives way, as a symbol of status, to the purchase of that which is new and fashionable. Patina in the modern world still functions to symbolize status but there are ways of cheating – such as buying that which is already old – which mean that it no longer works as a simple indicator of social status. McCracken unusually does discuss practices of ownership that involve an embodied relationship with the objects. He describes a series of rituals that sustain meaning (e.g. 'grooming rituals' – the cleaning and maintenance of objects such as the car) and erase meaning ('divestment rituals' – redecorating a house to divest traces of the previous owners). But his discussion of interaction with material objects and with their significance in material civilization is restricted to their symbolic value which, as is the case with most commentators on consumption, is simply to do with social status. The complexity of material life is not explored even in this context; is there any possibility of intrinsic pleasure to be derived from contact with these objects? Perhaps engagement with objects that are well fashioned of attractive materials provides its own enjoyment, perhaps contact with objects that have a biography that parallels that of the family is also important in terms of identity and belonging (see Dant 2001). And the practices of living with such objects may not simply be rituals that mark status but involve practical problems that may affect how they are enjoyed. For example, patina may be too rapidly acquired if the family silver is treated roughly or it may be obscured by being polished too eagerly.

'Use' and 'enjoyment' involve social and cultural processes that go beyond the symbolic display of social status What we choose to eat our meal off, whether it is a silver, china, glass, plastic or paper plate depends on the material culture we live in as well as the economic and cultural resources we have available. Our choice will also be linked to other aspects of material culture – such as cutlery, tables, dishwashers – as well as to the practices of food preparation and serving that we plan to use. But further, it will be linked to the occasion, the social event that the meal recognizes. The plate that is appropriate for a ceremonial meal or a family occasion may well be different from the one we feel comfortable with for a picnic or a TV dinner.

While social status may always be an issue in consuming for use and enjoyment, emotional, practical and other cultural factors both inform and shape our choices. Whatever the range of factors that bear on our choices, what is central is what we actually *do*; what plate we use and what practices it entails (polish it, put it in the dishwasher or throw it in the bin). It is the lived materiality of our bodies interacting with the materiality of objects that generates social significance of a range of types. The specificity of objects and actions both reflects and generates cultural conventions but significance is always limited by the practical and material constraints of our bodies and the objects they interact with.

Material civilization

There is a strand of thought within French social theory that takes a rather different view of the significance of material culture that will affect the argument of this book. In Chapter 4 I will refer to the writing of Mauss, Parlebas and Warnier from within anthropology, Tisseron within psychoanalysis, Latour and his colleagues within sociology and, in Chapter 5, most importantly I will refer to that of Merleau-Ponty from within philosophy. In French writing on consumption there is a similar emphasis on the representation of social status through some form of conspicuous consumption, as discussed above (e.g. Baudrillard 1981, 1998; Bourdieu 1984). However, there is at the same time an interest in the practices by which consumption is realized and how material culture is appropriated (e.g. Baudrillard 1996; Bourdieu 1990). Most commentators treat status as a simple continuous hierarchy; Bourdieu's (1984) very significant contribution was to introduce a lateral dimension so that taste in consumption could be used to more finely discriminate between class fractions that enjoyed different amounts of economic and cultural capital. But Bourdieu's rather problematic concepts of habitus and practice open up the potential for studying embodied relationships with the material stuff of life (1984, 1990).[8] Baudrillard's analysis of atmosphere and the sensuous engagement with materials such as wood and glass also points to the lived-with nature of material culture beyond its simply significatory or social status functions (1996). Other theorists of consumption within this French tradition such as Lefebvre (1971, 1991a, 2002) and de Certeau (1984) have also touched on the practical dimensions of lived relationships with material objects. De Certeau's collaborative work (1998) provides an exemplary and detailed empirical account of some of the practices of everyday life that are both material and embodied and at the same time linguistic and communicative.

There is in this body of work a theme of a developing and changing material civilization through modernity that is not dependent on the importance of signification and status. This theme is exemplified in the work of Fernand Braudel who provides an historical overview of material civilization that points to the limitations in the traditionally economistic perspective of the sociological approach I have discussed in previous sections. Writing in 1979, Braudel proposed an approach to history that did not overlook the complexities of economic life in the way that he felt that traditional economic history had. Instead of the traditional approach that saw the development of pre-industrial Europe as a 'gradual progress towards the rational world of the market, the firm and capitalist investment' (1992: 23), he wanted to draw attention to the routine, everyday activities of ordinary people that amounted to the production of economic wealth and also to the consumption of goods. Traditional economics had focused on the institutions of the market, the firm, banks, the state and the developing forms of capitalist investment such as the joint stock company. Even Marx had focused on the mode of production and the transformations at an institutional level of 'money' and 'capital' that had brought about wage labour, the factory and the alienation of workers from the means of production.

Braudel wanted to turn the attention of economic history to something more basic and practical that involved not just the capitalist and the worker, but everyone, including those on the margins of formal production such as children, women at home and people who were sick or elderly or disabled. The lives of all these people together constituted a 'rich zone, like a layer covering the earth, I have called for want of a better expression *material life* or *material civilisation*' (Braudel 1992: 23).

Braudel does not prioritize the zone of material civilization but argues that it must be recognized as contributing to the economic history of societies. He proposes a dialectical approach that will consider the market economy, the actions of key economic actors as well as the material life of everyone else. The mechanisms of capitalism are not to be found at any one level of economic processes but need to be understood as flowing between them. To shift the emphasis away from traditional economic concerns with the market and decisions by states, cartels and corporations, Braudel begins his three-volume history of economic development by setting out the changes in material civilization between the fifteenth and eighteenth centuries. His account of the development of different dimensions of material life – demography, food, costume, lodging, technology, money and towns – provides the background for the account in later volumes of what are more usually recognized as economic activities (Braudel 1992: 27). Braudel's history shows the very slow progress of material civilization over three centuries because there was no pressing need for change. He inherited from the earlier *Annales* historians Fevbre and Bloch, a broad-ranging approach that addressed changes over long periods of time (the *longue durée*, the epoch) and across different cultures, and his survey shows that while the pace of change varied in different parts of the world, it was often only slightly different and with relatively little impact. Braudel was keen not to focus on the lives of the wealthy as Veblen and Sombart had done, but to pay attention to local ways of doing things and the ordinary material life for most people. There were changes and innovations that had local rather than global impact and there was often a chain reaction as changes in one sphere of life affected changes in another. This process of gradual and incremental change in material civilization, having lasted for three centuries, began to speed up during the eighteenth and nineteenth centuries as the impact of industrialization spread throughout material life.

For example, water has always been a central component in the material life of human societies and as civilization has developed so there have been changes in the way that water has been drawn into that life. In early modern Europe there were fountains, aqueducts and cisterns before the Industrial Revolution but they were few and far between and technically very limited (Braudel 1992: 228–31). Traditional societies had, however, been built around water and towns and cities had developed from early settlements which were close to a substantial supply of running water. For early settlements and right through to the Industrial Revolution, rivers had been a key source of drinking water but larger settlements had also needed sufficient volume to provide water for cleaning, washing and the removal of waste products. Rivers had also been a means of transport as well as inter-rupting cross-country routes of travel. In Braudel's approach to history, the importance of a material such as water is linked to how a city can grow, how its food culture develops, how agriculture evolves and how labour is used. He discusses, for example, how prior to the Industrial Revolution 20,000 carriers earned their living carrying Seine water to Parisians for drinking. The river water was of course polluted as it was used for bathing and its banks were an open lavatory (Braudel 1992: 310). Nonetheless, Seine water was 'considered excellent for health' while at the same time being 'sup-posed to bear boats well' because it was muddy and therefore heavy (Braudel 1992: 229). The river water was treated as a natural purgative, although foreigners found it unpleasant, and it was regarded as much tastier than the well water from the left bank. Daniel Roche (2000), an his-torian who continues Braudel's approach to understanding material civi-lization, explains how the quality of local well-water affected, among other things, the taste of the bread. The waste water that Parisians threw out soaked down through cesspools, latrine ditches, gutters and graveyards to infiltrate and contaminate the underground water and there were disputes about the source of water – river, well or fountain – that should be used for bread-making (Roche 2000: 148–9). Steam pumps began to appear towards the end of the eighteenth century and during the nineteenth century a rapid series of developments separated polluted and fresh water. These tech-nological changes were linked to demands for improved hygiene and increasing recognition that pollution of the drinking water was responsible for cholera epidemics and the quasi-endemic typhoid. Different ways of drawing and using water, whether privately owned or shared, affected social arrangements: 'The collective wells in streets and squares, the private wells in urban courtyards brought together every day, just as in villages, neigh-bours of both sexes, servants, users of all kinds' (Roche 2000: 149).

The transformation of the way that water is moved and used has con-tinued apace since industrialized technology began to provide Paris with a clean and uncontaminated supply of fresh water and the safe removal of soiled water over the course of the nineteenth century. Since that time, those who live in the industrialized and wealthy world have come to take water for granted; it flows from the taps in our homes and is abundant for all the pleasures and uses we can incorporate it into. We can buy electric fountains for the garden, paddling pools for the children, automatic water-ing and sprinkling systems for flowerbeds and greenhouses along with hoses and high pressure jets for cleaning everything from the car to the stonework on the patio. In the house we can have automatic washing machines, dishwashers, power showers, baths, multiple sinks and 'water closets' and a central heating system based on hot water circulated in radiators – all drawing water from an apparently inexhaustible mains supply. Although we have grown up with this ready availability of water, in the past 50 years material civilization has evolved as we use more water than our parents' generation; we have more showers, deeper baths, put more water on our gardens, wash our cars more often and feel more indignant when tap water becomes contaminated or the supply is interrupted for some reason. During the twentieth century the capacity to dam, store and pump water long distances has increased so that our state bureaucracies can plan to create housing developments, hotels and green spaces (such as golf courses) where none would have been possible in the past. But this is an increasingly invisible and privatized material culture of water and the social life of the well has disappeared as the delivery of water has gone underground to emerge in each separate home. Roche describes how just a couple of centuries ago the smell of an unwashed body indicated prosperity and says that 'the French, associating strong smell with good health, kept up a long-lasting collective distrust regarding all ablutions' (2000: 158). Today our cultural values have reversed so that the unwashed body stands out offensively in the crowd of frequently washed and fragrant bodies.

As we read these historians of everyday material life, we are struck by how different everyday life was just a couple of hundred years ago. But, Braudel points out, although the ideas of Voltaire's age would not be so different from the ideas of our own, his material life would contrast dramatically (1992: 27–8). Braudel's work shows how with the coming of industrialization, material civilization changed dramatically after the slow and steady pace of earlier historical evolution – we only need to contrast his descriptions with our experience of the world we know today and its recent history. It is remarkable that the process of material civilization – which has carried on at a stunning pace throughout the twentieth century and of which water is only a small aspect – has largely been overlooked by sociology. The classical sociologists tried to grasp some of the sociological impacts of the economic upheavals that came with industrialization but they largely overlooked the detail of the changes in material life which also have social consequences. Braudel does not try to analyse the social impact of material civilization, he takes his task as merely to note the changes in material life that occurred during the pre-modern period, the centuries of industrialization and capitalism. His interest is in how material life underpins economic relations rather than social relations, although Roche explains that the group of French historians surrounding the journal *Annales* – Lucien Febvre, Robert Mandrou, Guy Thuillier and Fernand Braudel – used the theme of everyday material life to develop earlier historians' understanding of the process of civilization (Roche 2000: 3–5). The *Annales* historians questioned the economists' model of *homo oeconomicus* and instead adopted anthropological methods to observe the individual and collective practices and actions of ordinary people in order to under-stand civilization. The sociological reader will recognize *homo oeconomicus* as precisely the bugbear that Baudrillard attacks in his *Consumer Society* (1998) and Roche goes on to mention the *Annales* historians' attention to the topics of memory, communication, attitudes and habits that constitute culture through ordinary lives as expressed in Bourdieu's (1984) concept of 'habitus'.

Braudel's concept of 'material civilization' is a way of understanding how societies cohere through the ordinary interaction between our bodies and the material culture given to us by the society we live in:

> For civilisations do indeed create bonds, that is to say an order, bringing together thousands of cultural possessions effectively dif-ferent from, and at first sight even foreign to, each other – goods that range from those of the spirit and the intellect to the tools of everyday life.
>
> (Braudel 1992: 560)

As an approach to history, the idea of material civilization enabled Braudel to connect the detail of ordinary lives to the slow but continuous flow of history and to a broad geographic range of social experiences. It enabled him to argue with Weber and Sombart that the rationality of accounting methods and the moral distaste of usury were far from originating in a Protestant, European tradition that could be linked to the emergence of capitalism, because they had arisen in Catholic and Arabic cultures centuries earlier and had later been transported to Protestant European ones (Braudel 1982). And against Marx, with whom he had much more sympathy, he argued that capitalism was far more complex in its emergence than being the result of an economic transition from feudalism that followed an evolutionary logic of economic systems. Braudel had more in common with Marx's interest in the changes in the material life of industrialization in contrast to the ten-dency to emphasize the importance of ideas in the historical process.

Conclusion

In this chapter I have argued that the transition to modernity that was the focus of the classical sociologists was largely studied without taking account of the rapid and dramatic changes in material civilization that it brought. They focused on solidarity, sociality, rationality and political economy but paid little attention to the ordinary, practical, everyday, material life of the members of society who were experiencing this transition. How people get water, how they boil kettles, how often they wash are things that in the flow of everyday life are taken for granted. But it is precisely the changes in these material features of life that affect general well-being and health and have a direct impact on social relationships. I have argued that Marx's materialism did lead him to report the impact of changing practices of work on the material life of the working population and to make some remarks about the material civilization in general. But Marx had little to say about the use of commodities or about the effects of a developing material culture on the everyday life of the population. Simmel was more interested in the impact on material life of modern societies and how changes such as the typewriter, slotmachines and electric light were affecting the social subject and sociation in modern societies. Again, however, this is not a theme that is uppermost in Simmel's writing and it is one that is strikingly absent in the writings of Weber and Durkheim on the transition to modernity.

The classical sociologists had almost as little to say about consumption and the desire for commodities as they did about their use and effects, but a recent strand of work in history, anthropology and sociology has begun to fill in the missing component in the classical account of modernity by articulating the features and the importance of consumption. Some of the discourse around consumption has provided insights into developing the material civilization of modernity and, in an earlier book, I attempted to identify some of these different contributions to understanding the material culture in a social context (Dant 1999). However, the study of consumption has tended to focus either on the ways in which commodities are appropriated through buying and selling (advertising, shopping, desire for the new, the appeal to individual identity, etc.) or it has attempted to articulate consumption as a way of social structural alignment, through social class, emulation, ostentation and the habitus. Rewarding as these studies have been, they have often overlooked the mundane, routine ways in which material objects are taken up in everyday lives. Even when materiality is an issue in studies of consumption, as with McCracken's account of patina discussed above, it is treated primarily as a symbolic representation of social status.

How, then, to study material civilization in late modernity? how can we understand how objects mediate culture to people through the ordinary ways in which they use them? I do not intend to describe or survey the material civilization of late modernity as Braudel has done for its earliest stages because there is not sufficient social or historical distance for such an overview. Instead I will work towards developing an approach to material interaction that would be consistent with Marx's analysis of the impact of machines on working lives or Braudel's of the material life of an epoch, but would allow for more complexity and detail in understanding the flow of material life. But before I do, there are other discussions of materiality that can contribute to our understanding of materiality and sociality in late modernity.

3 Technology and modernity

Introduction

Following Braudel, I have suggested that material civilization is to do with the ordinary and everyday actions of people with objects – what I will call material interaction. As material civilization progresses, so the everyday life of human beings is changed by the increasing number and complexity of the human-designed and man-made objects that people interact with. I have argued that while Marx describes the impact of such objects on the process of production, sociology has largely had little to say about the significance of objects in social life. An exception is the sphere of technology which has attracted particular attention from philosophers and sociologists in the twentieth century. During the twentieth century technology brought about a dramatic and rapid change in the material life of people throughout the world but most particularly in the rich, industrialized West. As Donald Schön put it: 'A man of fifty in 1965 has seen too many changes in transportation, communication, warfare and industry to believe in the stability of technology' (1967: 200). Today we might put it that a woman of 50 has seen too many changes in all these things as well as in her everyday, personal and domestic life to believe that the materiality of human existence is stable. What were transformatory technologies in the middle of the twentieth century – the car, the television, military surveillance and machine-controlled production – have become ubiquitous throughout the western world and have transformed global relations. In the new millennium it is computer technology, the Internet, the mobile phone, genetic modification of crops, advances in surgery and the manipulation of fertility that provoke the view that technological change is characteristic of our society. As important as the changes themselves, however, is the increased likelihood that a man *or* a woman, of any social class would be enjoying these technological advances.

What is of significance for sociology is that the increasing tempo of technological change has changed the pace of material civilization and this has led critics to argue that technology has changed humankind's relationship with nature and the relationship between individual and society. Put simply, the critics suggest that technology has altered the human relationship with their material environment in ways that inhibit their full potential as human beings. In the sphere of social theory, these critiques have emphasized how the individual has become subordinated to a society driven by technology. At its most extreme, this is the argument that the shape of history in modernity is 'technologically determined', that is, that the form of society and the pattern of individual lives are determined by the objects that human beings have created. More interesting and persuasive, however, are the recurrent arguments around the theme that technology meets some human needs – for warmth, food, fuel, transport, entertainment, and so on – but at the cost of something essentially human that no machine can substitute for – imagination, creativity, ideas, passion, love. The debate is about the materiality of human existence that technology supports and the immateriality of human existence, its anima or soul, that technology threatens.

In this chapter I will discuss the work of some of the key critics of technology who are concerned about how it is shaping modern society and modern lives. It is Martin Heidegger's elliptical critique of how technology threatens the relationship between human beings and the world they live in that overshadows all later interventions that I shall discuss; Marcuse, Ellul, Winner, Hill and Feenberg. But I will begin with the prescience of Lewis Mumford's early comments that are remarkable in their anticipation so early in the century of the impact of technology that had not yet been imagined when he was writing.

Mumford

Lewis Mumford's *Technics and Civilization* (1934) was first drafted in 1930 and is a work of history and commentary with philosophical, religious and political overtones. Mumford's key theme is the significance of the 'machine' – which he distinguishes from a tool in its independence from the skill and motive power of its operator – in the technology of the early part of the twentieth century. A continuum runs from the hand tool manipulated by its operator to the automatic machine that runs more or less independently of any operator with variations in the application of motor power and control over tools.[1] The advance of technology is oriented to enhancing the quality of human life:

> In back of the development of tools and machines lies the attempt to modify the environment in such a way as to fortify and sustain

the human organism: the effort is either to extend the powers of the otherwise unarmed organism, or to manufacture outside of the body a set of conditions more favorable toward maintaining its equilibrium and ensuring its survival.

(Mumford 1934: 10)

Mumford is pointing to the centrality of technology to the *material* life of human beings, their embodied existence. Tools extend human capacity to meet material needs for clothing, shelter and warmth, while machines relieve humans of much of the physical effort of doing so and, in capturing in their design the capacity to form, also relieve humans of needing to replicate or continually perform with skill.[2] The history that Mumford writes about is how tools and machines have become central in human culture, shaping various parts of our lives, not only at work but at home and at leisure. It is, however, production that has led the way in drawing 'technics' into social and cultural development and Mumford refers to the connection of human relations, skills, tools, machines, apparatuses, and utilities that constitute a technological complex as 'the machine' (1934: 12). The civilization that emerges with the increasing adoption of technics is, however, not simply one in which the human organism is sustained by tools and machines. For Mumford, the modern, industrialized era of the twentieth century is one in which the flow of human life is even more 'disrupted' than in previous centuries because the machine has had effects that were not intended or planned. The clock provides a key trope for Mumford as a mechanical device that has had cultural effects far beyond its mechanical innovation as an object that incorporates precision engineering, standardization, automatic action and the containment and use of determinant amounts of power (1934: 14–15).[3] It has ordered time not just for machines but literally for everyone who wakes to the alarm clock and whose daily pattern of work, meals, travel and meetings is regulated according to the quantified segments of clock time. It is the interconnectedness of machines such as the clock with human practices and institutional systems that produces the technological complex of late modernity. Behind the use of electricity, for example, is a technical system of generation and distribution, not to mention the financial and administrative bureaucracy that is invisible to the user of an electric-powered machine but which is implicit in the availability of that machine for use when it is required. It is this embeddedness of machines within a technical infrastructure that is characteristic of the relation between technics and civilization in the twentieth century that Mumford describes as 'the machine'.

'The machine' has created what he calls a 'purposeless materialism', an excess of things, of the felt need to fill our lives with stuff. This is not the philosophical materialism of Marx, yet Mumford anticipates by some thirty years the critiques of consumerism offered by Marcuse (1991) and Baudrillard (1998):

> There is a disproportionate emphasis on the physical means of living: people sacrifice time and present enjoyments in order that they acquire a greater abundance of physical means; for there is supposed to be a close relation between well-being and the number of bathtubs, motor cars, and similar machine-made products that one may possess.
>
> (Mumford 1934: 273)

This is not a critique of materialism defined or driven by social status like Veblen's (1925) concept of 'conspicuous consumption'. This is a much more corrosive materialism that displaces the immaterial dimensions of life: fantasy, thought, imagination and creative effort. Instead of emotion leading to singing, it leads to putting on a record, instead of thoughts of a friend leading to imaginary conversation in reverie, it leads to picking up a telephone. This critique of the diminution of human capacities does have resonance with Simmel's critique of the effect of the typewriter that was mentioned in Chapter 2. For Mumford, the material means of consumer goods had become – as early as the 1930s – an end in themselves that was symbolic, not just of class status, but of 'intelligence and ability and of far-sightedness' (1934: 274). Goods were produced and consumed in excess of need or use as the habit of making more and fitting more stuff into life became standard cultural practice. His critique was not simply that these goods substituted for human capabilities but that they also modified human capacities so that photography, the telephone and the radio 'recultivated' the eye, the voice and the ear. There is here a transformation of the embodied, material relationship with the world that nonetheless has an impact on social relationships because it is the culture, the way of relating to other people in society, that is affected.

Now, for Mumford, these changes were both a threat to human nature and culture but also had potential for good beyond the easing of material life. Automation disconnected machines from human action, taking them out of the realm of continuous human control and thus breached the continuity with human intention. We can see this as an interruption of the 'intentional arc' that Merleau-Ponty traces between humans and the series of objects that they work with and on (see Chapter 5). But while machines threatened to displace the vital sensibilities of human beings, they also had the potential to enhance them. The machine brought new challenges to aesthetics as the environment became increasingly inhabited by machines and their products: 'But face to face with these new machines and instruments, with their hard surfaces, their rigid volumes, their stark shapes, a fresh kind of perception and pleasure emerges: to interpret this order becomes one of the new tasks of the arts' (Mumford 1934: 334).

Perhaps alone among critics of technology, Mumford recognizes the achievements of Cubist, Constructivist and Futurist artists in rising to this challenge and in Brancusi he finds the epitome of bringing together an aesthetic sensibility of organic material and form with an understanding of the potential of the machine to enhance and revise the possibilities of both. Mumford sees that the new machine arts threaten to displace more traditional handcrafts such as engraving or woodcutting, not least because the limited embodied skill required offers access to just about anyone. Photography, for example, may be much easier than woodcutting to acquire as a technical skill but that does not mean that all photographs share the same aesthetic value. The exceptional skill of photographers such as Alfred Stieglitz and Eugene Atget are able, he says, to 'restore to the eye … the stimulus of things roundly seen as things, shapes, colors, textures, demanding for its enjoyment a previous experience of light and shade, this machine process itself counteracts some of the worst defects of our mechanical environment' (Mumford 1934: 340).

Mumford's critique of technology is remarkable both in the specificity with which he records the shifts in material civilization over the previous millennium but also because he closely relates these changes to their impact on culture. His work offers a caution about the impact of machine technology in the past two hundred years, spelling out its threats to the working and personal lives of people, as well as the risks of a culture that has seemed frequently in thrall to each new invention. But his conclusion is that a 'dynamic equilibium' can be reached instead of the headlong rush to carve a linear history of technical progress (Mumford 1934: 430–1). He calls for three moments of balance that remain pertinent to any current critique of technology. The first is equilibrium between man and nature: conservation and restoration of soils, forests, minerals and metals. He also calls for reliance upon kinetic sources of energy (sun, falling water, wind), the recycling of metals and a restoration of over-urbanized metropolitan areas. The second is equilibrium between industry and agriculture where he argues against specialized farming for world export and in favour of mixed farming and market gardening for local production. Mumford hoped that this trend in agriculture would reflect the 'localism' of industry that followed the migration of technics from country to country and the absence of industrial focal points. His third moment of balance was for equilibrium in population growth which would involve migration away from those areas least equipped to support a large population to those rich and developed areas with the potential to do so. He would be saddened today to see how little balance in these areas had been achieved despite repeated calls along the same lines throughout the twentieth century.

Although *Technics and Civilization* remains Mumford's key contribution on the impact of technology on modern civilization, he wrote on many similar themes in later works, particularly *The Myth of the Machine* (1967). There he argues, in many ways against his own earlier work, that technics has played a much less significant part in the development of human civilization than it is usually given credit for. Both tool use and machine development were dependent on social and cultural capacities – most particularly language, aesthetic response and knowledge transmission – that are often overlooked in accounts of materiality. In distinguishing the emergence of human culture from merely animal modes of existence, his wide-ranging historical analysis identifies, as the archetypal machine, a device composed of human parts that he calls the 'megamachine':

> Only kings, aided by the discipline of astronomical science and supported by the sanctions of religion, had the capability of assembling and directing the megamachine. This was an invisible structure composed of living, but rigid, human parts, each assigned to his special office, role, and task, to make possible the immense work-output and grand designs of this great collective organisation.
>
> (Mumford 1967: 189)

The 'megamachine' is a sociological form, akin to Weber's bureaucracy, that involves power located in a single authority able to direct the intentional actions of a whole series of human beings to bring about transformations in the material environment. It was the technology of the 'megamachine' that built pyramids, castles, fortifications, aqueducts, tunnels and terraced agriculture long before contemporary mechanical technology began to transform the material world. That a coherent plan of material action is given legitimacy by a single authority and is then applied by the embodied actions of others has been the mode in which material civilizations have been shaped for millennia.

Questioning technology

Whereas Mumford begins with a long view of how technics contributes to civilization, Martin Heidegger begins his critique by thinking how human beings and objects come together in technology. In his essay, 'The question concerning technology' (1977a), originally delivered as a lecture in 1955, Heidegger challenges an instrumentalist account of technology that is based on causes and on means–ends relationships. Such an account appears, he says, so obvious as to appear 'correct' if not 'true' (Heidegger 1977a: 6) but by thinking through the process of traditional technology, that of manual, craft production in a workshop, he shows its limitations.

Heidegger uses the example of a silver chalice made for ritual purposes in which the causes that bring the object into being are fourfold: the material (silver), the form (chalice), the final purpose (a sacrificial rite) and that which brings about the effect (the silversmith). Rather than a linear, single causal chain, of means bringing about ends, causes are blended together to effect a 'bringing forth' or *poiēsis* which is also a 'revealing' as the chalice is brought forth into appearance by the 'occasioning' of the four causes. The silversmith is not the sole cause of the manufacture of the final object but is rather 'co-responsible', contributing the distinctive capacity for 'pondering' on the other three causes (Heidegger 1977a: 8). For Heidegger, technology is not a mechanical process of things causing others that can then simply be utilized instrumentally in the world by human beings, but is a more complex process of 'bringing forth', or 'revealing' that which is concealed, that is fundamental to the truth of Being: 'Technology is a mode of revealing. Technology comes to presence in the realm where revealing and unconcealment take place, where *alētheia*, truth, happens' (Heidegger 1977a: 13). Unlike the bringing forth of the natural world (the growth of plants, for example) technology involves knowledge. *Tekhnē* is a mode of knowing that includes forethought and planning, which anticipates the effects of the bringing forth through the fourfold process – the revealing of making depends on the prior revealing in anticipating what is to be made.

What Heidegger's critique resists are two ideas that are so often tied up with technology. First, that technology is simply the result of human ingenuity and instrumentality in manipulating the material world. He argues that the material world itself is involved in this process, providing possibilities and constraints, contributing to whatever is 'brought forth' or revealed by technological action. Second, Heidegger is arguing that *technology* is part of the process of Being-in-the-world which, as a consequence, is a much more subtle process than that which is either under the control of a single human or even of human beings as a collectivity or society. The *poiēsis* or 'bringing forth' that is technology is an aspect of human knowing of the world, of the confrontation between Dasein and her or his world that is prior to any specific culture or technological society. In traditional technology this takes the form of knowing 'how to' that is a practised and shared knowledge of how to transform the material world; knowledge precedes the action of materially changing the world. Modern technology extends this 'how to' knowledge to systematic, scientific knowledge that can anticipate what the end product will be and how it will fit into use. This type of knowledge may be in another person than the one who actually makes the thing, as happens when the designer of an object is quite independent of its manufacture. The other key feature of modern technology for Heidegger is the storing of energy that is released in the object (the hydroelectric dam, the aeroplane, the car). Like handcraft technology, modern technology is also, says Heidegger, a 'revealing' but one that is dependent on modern physics as an exact science. And this changes the character of 'bringing forth' to a 'challenging' that requires energy to be extracted and stored. Energy which is concealed in nature (in coal, in the heat of the sun) is unlocked, transformed, stored and distributed. This 'challenging' form of revealing takes on the characteristics of 'regulating and securing' and is subject to an 'ordering'. The process of extracting and storing energy is not haphazard but is managed according to a system which allows objects to be kept ready for use as a 'standing-reserve'. Such objects (e.g. an airliner) in standing-reserve are not simply held as 'stock' – they are ready to be put to use once the order changes.

The thrust of Heidegger's critique of the nature of modern technology comes when he questions man's orientation to its process. First, he argues that man has also become part of the standing-reserve – his example is the modern woodcutter who is made subordinate to a chain of order and challenge: cellulose, paper, newspapers. The technician in the modern garage (see Chapter 1, note 4), who works with hand tools and manages the work within his assigned job, is nonetheless in a chain of command, or a social order, that includes the foreman, the garage manager, the garage owners, the car manufacturers and their service specifications, the MOT, health and safety regulations, and so on. We can see that 'man' is standing-reserve challenged into the technical work of car repair and maintenance by a social system that precedes him and specifies him (his qualifications, his hours of work, rates of pay, etc.) in much the same way as the machine tools he works with. This is a long way from the craftwork of the silversmith making a chalice. Heidegger argues that 'man does not have control over unconcealment itself, in which at any given time the real shows itself or withdraws' (1977a: 18) – in other words, it would be supremely arrogant to claim that it was man that had brought about the nature of standing-reserve. Whatever is 'brought forth' depends not only on man and his intentions: 'The uncon-cealment of the unconcealed has already come to pass whenever it calls man forth into the modes of revealing allotted to him. When man, in his way, from within unconcealment reveals that which presences, he merely responds to the call of unconcealment even when he contradicts it' (Heidegger 1977a: 19). Here the intentional actions of human beings are constrained to operate within whatever technological system prevails, so that choice and creativity are severely curtailed. While the potency of modern technology extends human power over the material world as against traditional technology, the possibilities of 'unconcealment' are restricted to those modes or revealing 'allotted' by the paths of technology.

Modern technology is no 'mere human doing' says Heidegger, as he names the 'challenging claim' which 'gathers man' to 'order the self-revealing as standing-reserve "*Ge-stell*" [Enframing]' (1977a: 19). This way of describing the impact of modern technology both avoids any causal account or any simple historical or anthropological account which would see technology as the outcome of the combined effects of individual human ingenuity. As Loscerbo puts it: 'man, prior to all his ordering of nature in general, is himself *already* put to the challenge' (1981: 239), that is to say, *Gestell* is a property of Being. *Gestell* or 'enframing' here means more than giving a framework to – it invokes the idea of a calling forth, a gathering and a challenging claim (Heidegger 1977a: 19, fn17). Enframing is the essence of modern technology but it is much more than the range and variety of technologies available in the world. Indeed, *Gestell* is itself outside of technology, a quality of Being that becomes the driving force of technology and its adoption in the ordering activities of human beings. Its revealing concerns nature as the storehouse of the standing energy reserve and 'man's ordering attitude and behaviour display themselves first in the rise of modern physics as an exact science' (Heidegger 1977a: 21). The enframing that is the essence of modern technology is a dynamic that is prior to human control and thus is always beyond it and, as such, a 'danger' (Heidegger 1977a: 26).

We could say that the work of the modern garage is 'enframed' by the industrial complex of which it is a part. Rather than the modern car being a made object that is operated until it fails, it is designed to be maintained and repaired with regular inspections and the replacement of the oil, brake-pads, spark plugs, and so on, that significantly extend the life of the car. The work of the garage technician contributes to this enframing in that his skills in carrying out replacement of parts, in undertaking sequences of checks (for MOTs and for servicing) are already part of the 'revealing' that has been achieved by the modern automotive industry. Through both systematic testing and through experience accumulated in the business of maintaining cars, a set of routines have been established which will reduce the chances of the failure of the vehicle. The technicians' embodied, personal experience of cars and their workings, manifested as skill in their everyday work practice, operates within a context that shapes and moulds it; what is as important are the techniques and standards that are made available to the technician through training, through manuals[4] and through regimes for procedures issued by manufacturers or by the garage owners.[5]

For Heidegger, the enframing of modern technology takes the control for interaction with the material world out of the hands of the individual and embeds it in systems that are partly social and partly technical. And this produces the danger that humans do not realize that the process is beyond their control. The arrogance of humans means that they believe that they control technology, that it is their instrument to manipulate the material world. As social and political systems are established to steer technology, the complexity of the fourfold process of causation is easy to overlook (in a way that it isn't for the craftsman who constantly confronts his materials and who struggles to produce form). The creation of a standing-reserve produces the potential for massive damage or destruction and here lies the limitation of human beings' power to subordinate the material to their instrumentality by technology. The way that Heidegger analyses modern technology shows that it is 'enframing' that is its essence even although it is 'nothing technological'. It is a process of revealing or uncon- cealment that orders modern technology: 'In Enframing, that unconcealment comes to pass in conformity with which the work of modern technology reveals the real as standing-reserve. This work is therefore neither only a human activity nor a mere means within such activity' (Heidegger 1977a: 21). It is science that creates the distance between the real as standing-reserve and the human activities of technology. Science enables the planning and cali- bration of the effects of modern technology in advance of any work upon materials or form and thus alters the fourfold nature of causality. The human agent and the form of material objects become subordinate to the science that predicts how nature will respond and prescribes human inter- action with materiality. This is how enframing reveals the real as standing- reserve in a process that is larger than any individual can grasp and which 'starts man upon the way' and which Heidegger calls, in his gerund-forming style, 'destining' (1977a: 24). The danger in enframing is veiled and disguised and this is what is most worrying about it (1977b: 37). But in confronting the essence of technology through thinking, there is the possibility of a 'turning', a turn in, a turn homeward that makes clear the coming to pres- ence of Being: 'When, in the turning of the danger, the truth of Being flashes, the essence of Being clears and lights itself up' (Heidegger 1977b: 44). Thinking holds the possibility of bringing about 'insight into that which is' and disclosing the coming to presence of technology but Heidegger points out that certain modes of what in ordinary language we might call thinking are already technological – those calculative attempts to reckon on reality, the use of psychology to enumerate the symptoms of fate, the use of historiography to chart the future, are parts of technology and do not disclose the truth of Being.

Heidegger's critique does not call for a rebellion against modern tech- nology or a return to traditional technology. He does not offer any simple solution but argues that humans need to confront and engage with the process of technology through thinking rather than presuming it to be their instrument: 'So long as we do not, through thinking, experience what is, we can never belong to what will be' (1977b: 49). The 'destining' of modern technology is not determinative of humans' role in Being; it may suggest a route and offer a fate but not one that has to be obeyed blindly and without alternative. Heidegger refers to a hydroelectric plant on the River Rhine as one of his examples of modern technology; it is easy to recognize as a tech- nological project that requires far more than the 'how-to' knowledge with which a windmill might be built. Whereas the windmill takes advantage of the wind that it converts into the turning of grindstones for flour milling, it does not store it as energy (Heidegger 1977a: 14), whereas the hydroelectric plant stores the energy of moving water behind a dam that is released according to the need for electric power. The natural forces that are harnessed in the hydroelectric plant could not be managed without the planning of physical structures using a scientific understanding of the behaviour of materials and energy. The form of both the dam and the turbines are calculated in all their dimensions before building commences; the potential to generate power is known in advance. Once built, the water behind the dam can be held as a standing-reserve to be ordered by managing the flow in response to demands for electric power. Even before it is built, even before it is designed, the hydroelectric plant becomes a destiny for those who will be affected by it – as soon as it is agreed to build it. This may involve political and economic decisions that have to be made before technology is invoked. And once the decisions are made, the 'bringing forth' or 'revealing' that is technological activity seems to be destined by those decisions which are not themselves technological. We can understand this process as enframing in that it follows a pattern that seems to be set by the world rather than by design or technology.

What Heidegger's critique argues is that human freedom resides in looking and listening, which seems to suggest being willing to resist the destiny that appears to be set with the decision to build: 'For man becomes truly free only insofar as he belongs to the realm of destining and so becomes one who listens and hears, and not one who is simply constrained to obey' (1977a: 25). The danger lies in accepting the inevitability of destiny, of acceding to the impulsion to proceed down a path that appears to be a technological imperative, and takes two forms. First, of treating the individual as standing-reserve (the workers who die in the process of building the dam? those whose homes and livelihoods are destroyed by its building?); the other of treating the individual as 'lord of the earth', as being able to wield technology as their instrument (Heidegger 1977a: 27). But there is a 'saving power' that lies in the destiny of enframing, it is humans' capacity for knowledge, their desire for the truth through 'catching sight of what comes to presence in technology instead of merely staring at the technological' (Heidegger 1977a: 32). Perhaps this is what happens when we question the need for a new hydroelectric plant, when we explore what happened in the past with other such plants and consider the alternative ways of meeting the demand for more electric power. Science may be part of the bringing forth that is modern technology but it can also be used to resist what might appear to be technological imperatives; enframing brings with it both danger and 'saving power'.

Heidegger provides a critique of technology that questions whether it has developed in such a way that it restricts the potential for authentic being among humans. The technology of the early twentieth century – the aircraft, the hydroelectric dam, the car – affects all human existence by fundamentally changing the relationship between human beings and nature.

These types of technology seem to incorporate a 'logic' or irresistible path for future human action that determines a wide range of human actions (e.g. using aircraft as a standard means of transport, using electric power for many purposes) and supervenes in the consideration of alternative paths for human actions. Heidegger's interest is as a philosopher rather than as a sociologist or political commentator but later sociologically oriented critiques such as those of Ellul and Marcuse draw on both Mumford's historical critique of the emerging dominance of technology and Heidegger's argument that modern technology changed the relationship between human beings and the society in which they live.

Critical theory and technology – Marcuse

In the Frankfurt School tradition, Herbert Marcuse articulates a critique of technology that builds on Marx's analysis of the technological changes in the mode of production and draws on Heidegger's critique of the nature of existence. Like Marx, Marcuse sees that technological innovation in the process of production – the development of machine tools, production line assembly, automatic machines – increases the alienation of those who work with these machines. Unlike Marx, however, Marcuse emphasizes the extension of the principles of technology into the economy. For Marx, the logic of capitalism co-opted the potential of technology to enhance profits, promote capital accumulation and extend the control over the workforce, but for Marcuse, technology becomes a feature of capitalist economics itself.

Marcuse's account of 'technological rationality' as the logic of advanced capitalism develops, in a slightly different direction, the theme of 'instrumental reason' most explicitly articulated by Max Horkheimer. For Horkheimer, instrumental reason applied a particular form of thinking to the material world; reason that oriented means to specified ends. It entails something of Heidegger's concept of the instrumentality that lies behind technology, but in thinking of it as a mode of reason, of thought, of abstraction, it also captures something of Heidegger's concept of 'enframing', of a mode of bringing forth or revealing that is not itself technological. For Horkheimer, instrumental reason generated forethought and planning which created a material culture that increasingly bore the marks of modernity:

> The objects we perceive in our surroundings – cities, villages, fields and woods – bear the mark of having been worked on by man. It is not only in clothing and appearance, in outward form and emotional make-up that men are the product of history. Even the way they see and hear is inseparable from the social life-process as it has evolved over the millennia ... The sensible world which a member

of industrial society sees about him every day bears the marks of deliberate work: tenement houses, factories, cotton, cattle for slaughter, men, and in addition, not only objects such as subway trains, delivery trucks, autos, and airplanes but the movements in the course of which they are perceived. The distinction within this complex totality between what belongs to unconscious nature and what to the action of man in society cannot be drawn in concrete detail. Even where there is a question of experiencing natural objects as such, their very naturalness is determined by contrast with the social world and, to that extent, depends on the latter.

(Horkheimer 1999: 200–2)

The phrase 'instrumental reason' both captures the idea of reasoned thought being oriented towards instrumental ends and the idea that thought itself is an instrument applied to have a transformatory effect on the world. Marcuse's concept of 'technological rationality' (1998: 44) has slightly different connotations, suggesting that rationality lies not simply in processes of thought that use reason to progress towards specific goals but is also embedded in the practices of technology: techniques and technics, the ways that machines operate and constrain their interaction with human beings.

Marcuse argues that the pursuit of individual self-interest was allied to the principles of economic rationality until mechanization began to transform the nature of economic production with the effect of favouring 'giant enterprises of machine industry' (1998: 43). Technology favoured large economic organizations, undermining the interests of the individual at the same time as achieving a domination of nature. Independently powered machinery could transform natural materials at greater speed, with greater strength and quicker than any single individual or even groups of workers could achieve. In the place of the economic self-interest of the individual, a technical principle of efficiency, something that could be subject to calculation independently of the individual's entrepreneurial skills, was applied to the process of production. This techno-economic logic favoured large organizations and ones that maximized their mechanical efficiency through the use of whatever technology was available and applicable. In setting out the principles under which advanced capitalism was emerging, Marcuse showed how it was steered by a technologically oriented 'apparatus'. The 'apparatus' was neither the economic machinery of capitalism, nor just the firm, or corporation. As well as these institutions, it also included the 'devices' and organizational features characteristic of an industry (Marcuse 1998: 44, fn6): techniques, machine tools, routine strategies and processes. The human practices had been developed alongside machines as part of the research and development efforts that were beginning to become an established part of industrial production early in the twentieth century. Instead of a form of thought, instrumental reason, generating the apparatus, Marcuse's 'technological rationality' was generated by the apparatus which was both social and technical – rather like Heidegger's enframing. The mode of calculative and objective thought of instrumental reason had become materialized in machines, machine processes, work practices oriented to machines and bureaucratic structures. Marcuse argued that it was the apparatus that determined the form and kind of commodities that were to be produced and at the time that he was writing – during the rapid economic gearing up of the United States during the Second World War – this was a reasonable analysis. However, long before the end of the twentieth century, feedback mechanisms responding to the practices of consumption had been built into the production process (market research, focus groups, product testing) so the 'apparatus' has been extended into the consuming side of everyday life (Baudrillard 1998).

The problem with the technological rationality of the apparatuses of modern societies is, for Marcuse, that they suppress individuality. Drawing on other critics of technology such as Marx, Veblen and Mumford, he points out that the human operator becomes subordinate to the automatic machine as its assistant or attendant. This makes work more 'matter of fact', requiring less thought, spontaneity or imagination and the routinization of the material life of people at work turns them into a mass or collective and suppresses their individuality. Rather like Heidegger and Mumford, Marcuse is careful to point out that this is not a consequence of technology itself but the way that technology becomes embedded in the social organization of advanced capitalism: 'Technics hampers individual development only insofar as they are tied to a social apparatus which perpetuates scarcity, and this same apparatus has released forces which may shatter the special historical form in which technics is utilized' (Marcuse 1998: 63). The very mode of collective action under technological rationality could inhibit technical development as workers are less likely to use their imagination to solve practical problems. Instead, management, especially 'scientific management' becomes the vehicle of technological rationality in which human practices are subject to a quantitative and comparative technical analysis – the same impersonal methods are applied to machines and humans alike. The embodied material practice of workers – their ability to interact freely with objects following the intentionality embedded in the object – is curtailed as behaviours and routines become rationalized, standardized and specified.[6]

In *One-Dimensional Man* ([1964] 1991) Marcuse extends this analysis from the institutions and technology of the 'apparatus' of production, to the technology of consumption and everyday life. What Heidegger calls 'enframing', Marcuse calls the 'introversion' of technological rationality into embodied practice that affects everyday life relationships with material objects, shifting individuals' sensibility away from their emotional and mental lives towards what he calls the 'objective order of things' (Marcuse 1991: 147). In place of the dialectical play between Eros and Logos traditionally characteristic of knowledge, technological rationality generated a one-dimensional style of thought characterized by 'false consciousness' as it became suborned to a 'growing technical ensemble of things and relations which included the technical utilization of men' (Marcuse 1991: 149). The rewards for participating in advanced capitalist society were material, a higher standard of living expressed in terms of access to things in the way Mumford had described. But for Marcuse, the material of consumption carried with it ideological connotations so that:

> The means of mass transportation and communication, the commodities of lodging, food, and clothing, the irresistible output of the entertainment and information industry carry with them prescribed attitudes and habits, certain intellectual and emotional reactions which bind the consumers more or less pleasantly to the producers and, through the latter, to the whole. The products indoctrinate and manipulate; they promote a false consciousness which is immune against its falsehood.
>
> (Marcuse 1991: 14)

In accepting the rationality of advanced capitalism, individuals consume to create a material life that they feel reflects their personal needs. What they overlook is how technological rationality has created a social mass whose material needs are basically the same – while each individual in the mass perceives them as personal and tied to their sense of identity and difference. Consumption generates conformity and restricts criticism; once production has been organized according to the principles of technological rationality, then the cultural acquiescence of consumers was all that was needed for the emergence of one-dimensional society.

Marcuse's solution to the problem is not so far from Heidegger's 'thinking'; Marcuse wants to see a restimulation of thought and criticism incorporating a 'reconciliation of Logos and Eros' that might lead to liberation (Marcuse 1991: 171). Like Heidegger and Mumford before him, he recognizes that technological development cannot be reversed, material civilization cannot be made to go backwards, but Marcuse wants to invoke a subversive mode of thought that could embrace the negative and the irrational to counterbalance scientific reason and thus lead to human liberation. However, he recognizes the capacity for technological rationality to absorb and dispel the power of negative thought in a 'harmonization' that would not be liberatory. One example of this process that he sets out is this:

> I ride in a new automobile. I experience its beauty, shininess, power, convenience – but then I become aware of the fact that in

a relatively short time it will deteriorate and need repair; that its beauty and surface are cheap, its power unnecessary, its size idiotic; and that I will not find a parking place. I come to think of *my* car as a product of one of the Big Three automobile corporations. The latter determine the appearance of my car and make its beauty as well as its cheapness, its power as well as its shakiness, its working as well as its obsolescence. In a way, I feel cheated. I believe that the car is not what it could be, that better cars could be made for less money. But the other guy has to live, too. Wages and taxes are too high; turnover is necessary; we have it much better than before. The tension between appearance and reality melts away and both merge in one rather pleasant feeling.

(Marcuse 1991: 230–1)

This example nicely presents the dilemma of the modern liberal. We know that we are caught up in a material society that is both seductive and repellent, that provokes positive and negative feelings, that we are ultimately ambivalent about. We are realistic about the nature of commodities and consumer society, can see through advertisements and are reluctant to trust the material goods on which our daily lives depend. In Marcuse's example the ambiguity of feeling about the car and its origins is not all felt at once; its beauty is felt in one moment (as we wash or polish it), its imminent decline in another (when it fails to start). But Marcuse's point is that what might seem to be a negative, critical, moment, what appears to be a dialectical response to the materiality of advanced capitalism, is in fact simply an obfuscation of the distinction between rational appearance and irrational reality. The negation is absorbed within the positive to produce a harmony – we continue to live with the car. Indeed, the negative responses to the car have fed into the progress of consumer society; during the latter half of the twentieth century cars got smaller, lower power options were offered, bodywork was dipped to resist rusting, workers earned higher wages – better cars were made for less money. This is how the materiality of everyday relations between human beings and the things around them has improved but within the logic of technological rationality and advanced capitalism. If there is a risk that harmonization of the negative will allow the enduring dominance of technological rationality, Marcuse also recognizes that technics itself can be used to undermine it. Technology, he said, 'has rendered possible the satisfaction of needs and the reduction of toil – it remains the very base of all forms of human freedom' (Marcuse 1991: 236). All that would be needed to make technology work for liberation would be a critical approach to the application of technics that identified the 'discrepancy between the real and the possible, between the apparent and the authentic truth' (Marcuse 1991: 233).

The technological society – Ellul

If Marcuse's analysis of the changing relationship between society and materiality is informed by the critiques of Marx and Heidegger, Jacques Ellul ([1954] 1965) arrives at many similar conclusions from an altogether different route that draws on a religious conception of the essence of human being. From an analysis of how technique[7] had migrated from the machine to human practices, he argues that modern societies had become during the twentieth century 'technological societies'. Administrative and organizational practices have come to be modelled on the principles of the machine in which goals are specified and the efficacy of means is calculated. Plans and standardized procedures follow what has been systematically learnt and practices and procedures are set out in advance based on their calculated effects. Techniques modelled on the efficient machine had come to be applied in cultural practices such as political administration, police power, medicine, pedagogy, and propaganda that make 'man himself the object of technique' (Ellul 1965: 22). A form of human engineering had emerged as advertising, propaganda and personal relations techniques were applied in fields such as sport and medicine, helping to create a mass culture and suppress the critical faculty of individual thought so that 'the human being becomes completely incapable of escaping the technical order of things' (Ellul 1965: 396–7). This concern with the effects of technique on consciousness parallels Marcuse's criticism of the effects on the media, managerial psychology, therapy and language that absorb technological rationality (see e.g. Marcuse 1991: 88–93, 110–11, 200–1). In a similar vein, Ellul points to how the techniques of education, counselling and vocational guidance utilize strategies that have worked with material technology at the same time as serving to bend humans to compliance with that technology (1965: 344–63). Although techniques had been applied for millennia in narrow, local spheres of action, the process of industrialization had seen their spread through all aspects of life with little political or religious resistance – what is lost is spontaneity and authentic individuality.

Ellul provides a rather different emphasis from previous critiques by arguing that it is the impact of technological society on the range of possible practical and spiritual actions of individuals that is curtailed by the prescribed and automatic actions characteristic of technological society. Technique invades all dimensions of modern life, transforming the nature of work, of war, and domestic life. It reduces the physicality of human action, reducing the degree of contact with physical environment, transforming human bodily engagement with space, time and with speed. The pilot of the supersonic aircraft provides a vivid example of this material transformation of human being:

The pilot of the supersonic aircraft at its maximum velocity becomes, in a sense, completely one with his machine. But immobilized in a network of tubes and ducts, he is deaf, blind and impotent. His senses have been replaced by dials which inform him of what is taking place. Built into his helmet, for example, is an electro-encephalographic apparatus which can warn him of an imminent rarefaction of oxygen before his senses could have told him. We can say he 'subsists' in abnormal conditions; but we cannot say he is adapted to them in any real human sense. And his situation is not exceptional.

(Ellul 1965: 325–6)

The supersonic pilot's embodied experience of technology is still quite exceptional (it was even more so in 1964) but the progressive incorporation of human bodily existence into technology has indeed developed along the lines Ellul indicates. The modern car driver, for example, is distanced from the external environment as climate and sound are technologically managed. The ubiquitous lights and dials on the dashboard have been supplemented in many modern cars by warning sounds, video-assisted reversing, and 'head-up' displays projected onto the windscreen. Automatic systems – such as ABS, self-adjusting suspension systems, light-sensitive headlights, responsive power-steering, and so on – can mediate the interaction between driver, the road and the world they live in.

As if picking up Heidegger's example of the hydroelectric dam and Marcuse's suggestion that technology shapes ideology, Ellul uses the Tennesse Valley Authority (TVA) as an example of how technology becomes ideology. As well as generating hydraulic power and distributing it to the neighbouring localities, the TVA became a symbol of regionalism, decentralizing the political power of public and private, federal and local institutions (Ellul 1965: 323). But the hydroelectric dam also illustrates how nature is suborned to technology: 'Just as hydroelectric installations take waterfalls and lead them into conduits, so the technical milieu absorbs the natural. We are rapidly approaching the time when there will be no longer any natural environment' (Ellul 1965: 79).

As thought is separated from action, technique becomes ubiquitous, colonizing not only the consciousness of modern people but also their spirit: 'The very assimilation of ideas into the technical framework which renders them materially effective makes them spiritually worthless' (Ellul 1965: 425). Technique has had beneficial effects not only in offering freedom from famine and the opportunity of leisure but also in combating inequities such as slavery. There may be ways of making techniques more applicable to human beings rather than simply demanding human beings to adapt. But what seems more likely to Ellul, anticipating the impact of gene technology by many years, is that technique will produce a 'superman' through chemical means and even 'embryonic conditioning' that will be better able to resist the vagaries of material existence (1965: 337). Overall, technological society is no better than any previous society because material gains must be weighed against losses in terms of the spiritual and emotional dimensions of human being. Technological society is here to stay so all that can be hoped for is to bring technique and the continued existence of human being into harmony by one of two means (Ellul 1965: 429–30). The first is to generate new techniques that do not stand apart or in opposition to the human being but blend more closely with its capacities. Writing in the very earliest days of computer technology, Ellul suggests that the development of 'thinking machines' could be such a way forward. The second is that we might rethink what it is to be a human being, adapting our conception of human existence to take into account the changed material circumstances of technological society.

Technology in control?

There are a number of recurring themes in the critique of the relationship between technology and society. One of them is the call for humanizing the relationship, shifting the balance from technique back towards a more distinctively human dynamic of imagination and spontaneity that is not replicated in technological systems, whether human or mechanical. This theme emerges in all the critics I've mentioned in this chapter and it recurs in later commentators. Donald Schön (1967), for example, bemoans the socio-cultural effect of technology in stabilizing systems so that they inhibit ingenuity in creating new practices and indeed new technologies. Rather than a stolid linear process of social progression dominated by technological systems that he calls the 'Technological Program of Modernity', Schön proposed an 'ethic of change' that would accept the decline of stability and embrace a phenomenological approach to invention that 'demands starting from where, in fact you are – not where you thought you were … It requires priority for the here and now … the priority of immediate experience' (1967: 206). His calls for including the openness to change of the inventor and the artist echo Marcuse's emphasis on the aesthetic dimension in modernity and Heidegger's on the importance of thinking.

   These critics are responding to the passing of cultures that were dominated by a religious order of belief, in which technology was subordinate to spiritual ideals. Modernity, and the industrialization that has accompanied it, on the one hand, deposed God as the arbiter of value and, on the other, replaced Him with the mundane value of technology that follows that pragmatic principle – 'does it work?' Science has provided a systematic hermeneutics of the lived-in world that if it does not exactly generate technology, nonetheless legitimates and explains it, providing an ideological support that enables modern technology to harness the resources of a whole society, as with the building of hydroelectric plants, space travel or the development of networked technologies (telephones, computers, power systems, water systems). It is with the move of technology out of mere material arrangements into the systematic planning of material and social projects that modern technology emerges and threatens to become an autonomous and self-directing force. Human social arrangements, as all the critics remark, come to be designed according to a mode of thought that is materialist before it is human or spiritual. This appears to be the destiny of the technological societies that have emerged in the twentieth century, where materiality precedes sociality and where the pace of change speeds up as technology drives the culture to constantly catch up.

Another recurrent theme in the critique of technology is that of the automatic machine, one that acts on its own to transform the material world, apparently independent of direct human intention. This theme, that we can see in Marx's, Mumford's, Marcuse's and Ellul's response to technology, threatens ultimately to remove the human element altogether. In Langdon Winner's scary phrase, it is not the automatic machine that threatens the humanity of society but 'Autonomous Technology' (1977). This is one aspect of the 'danger' that Heidegger warns us about; the fear of man-made objects is extended to include a fear of the social organizations that incorporate them. It is more than reasonable to fear a machine over which human beings have lost control; the airplane in which the mechanical controls fail or the car whose driver is drunk or passes out are very unpredictable and dangerous objects. But what becomes really scary is when such dangerous machinery is put in the hands of a technical organization that seems to operate in an autonomous and unaccountable way. The paradigm case halfway through the twentieth century was the nuclear bomb whose awesome power not only could kill vast numbers of people – some very slowly – but also devastate landscapes, making them hideous and uninhabitable. The threat of these types of objects to the materiality of our world and our lives is of course intended but they are 'safe' as long as they are either used properly or, in the case of nuclear weapons, never used at all. The issue becomes one of control. Sufficient technical safeguards and rational political systems should ensure that the deterrent effect maintains a status quo, a balance of power that controls such objects and does not use them. But can the political and technical systems ever be deemed truly 'fail-safe'?

During the latter half of the twentieth century another type of concern has emerged about the unintended consequences of ordinary technology designed to enhance the material conditions of existence. The polluting effects of technology designed to enhance mobility (particularly by air and by motor vehicle) threatens our material environment in a variety of ways with both short-term and long-term impacts. The effects of major schemes, such as those for generating nuclear and hydroelectric power, are recognized to be far more complex than was originally thought. The consequences of genetic modification of crops, of genetic alteration of human cells and even the social and cultural impact of innovations in reproductive technology, are difficult, if not impossible, to anticipate. Underlying these fears about specific technologies is a fear that technology as a social system has become self-producing, taking on a life of its own, directed by its own logic of cumulative innovation and thus independent of the control of humankind.

Winner explores this fear that human beings have lost mastery of their world but reminds us that the whole point of technology, whether mechanical or social in form, is that it should determine at least some aspects of human existence. Technology works precisely when and because it determines either some material event in the world or some human action. Whether it is a machine or a technical organization, the whole point is to produce a definite and predictable outcome: 'technology succeeds through the conquest of disorder and the imposition of form' (Winner 1977: 75). We cannot have technology without some measure of technological determinism and without ceding some human autonomy to the technology as the intended choice of human actors. However, Winner recognizes that technology brings unchosen and unintended consequences, such as the atmospheric pollution generated by the car's internal combustion engine and the accidental injury to road users. Often those who suffer unintended consequences are not those who intentionally put the technology into use. Car drivers gain mobility but cyclists are more likely to experience death or injury without any gain. More complicated still are those victims of the damaged environment, both now and in the future, who are separated in space and time from any gains from the technology that caused the damage.

Winner suggests that one of the reasons that technology has become so potent in modernity is precisely because it exceeds our intentions and produces unintended consequences. Provided that there is a sufficient material reason to proceed, then the unintended consequences will be treated as a necessary evil or, as is often the case, will be found to be beneficial and will be embraced: 'Each new variety of apparatus, technique or organization expands the sphere of human possibilities to a degree which, in the nature of things, remains uncertain' (Winner 1977: 98). The example Winner uses is the computer; if it had been treated as nothing more than a calculating machine, then we would not have the flexible communications and information storage devices we have today. The unintended consequences of computing power were seized upon and developed without regard for the originating intentions behind the device. The effect, Winner argues, is to produce 'technological drift' rather than a trajectory of development that is either reducible to human intentions or to determination from within 'technique' or 'technological rationality'. History, technological development and cultural change cannot be specified as 'determined' either by the human mind or the material constitution of the world. Both interact together in shaping change that is manifest both in the material world and the social world.

The politics of technology is tied up with issues about who gains, who loses, how a balance can be made and by the difficulty in differentiating between human and material elements within these systems. The politics is made more complicated by the way that different technologies (say, electronics and aircraft building) become entangled in technological systems in which what are in fact human interests may appear as a technological imperative. Winner points out how this can lead to what he calls 'reverse adaptation': 'the adjustment of human ends to match the character of available means' (1977: 229) which is exactly the sort of danger envisaged by Heidegger, Marcuse and Ellul. Rather than technology being designed to solve practical problems, we adapt to what has been invented – just think of the mobile phone – and the socio-technical system does its best to encourage us in our adaptation. Design is not the consequence of simply articulated human intention but the result of the interaction of sub-systems within a technological system. Winner argues that the politics of technology is about the way that technological systems become self-controlling – autonomous – through the effects of reverse adaptation. These systems can control markets, political regulation, institutional aims as well as creating and extending 'needs' and crises (Winner 1977: 241–51). The technology does not act as an independent agent but within a social situation it *appears* as if it is such an agent with its own imperatives. The political context that might aspire to control technological systems involves a variety of competing interests, some of which are tied into the system and others of which may be ignorant of the consequences of a technology. As Winner accepts, interests and knowledge are connected but both are also affected by education and class status.

There are, however, 'megatechnical systems' in which the personal and social interests of individuals, groups and classes are subordinated to or co-opted by a 'technological imperative' in which 'a chain of reciprocal dependency is established in which the various aspects of a given technical operation overlap and require each other' (Winner 1977: 101). These aspects include the dependence of advanced technologies on other technologies and on material and economic resources. For example, to be a socially useful means of transport, the automobile requires manufacture, repair, fuel supply, highways, and so on. The technological imperative overrides group interests, Winner claims, because whatever group is making the decisions is forced to follow the pragmatic requirements of the technological imperative. Until you have a viable alternative to the motor car, you have to keep investing in the road system to enable people to get to work; otherwise the economy grinds to a halt with socially disastrous consequences. The technological imperative becomes more potent, the more complex, far-reaching and interdependent that technological systems become. The agency that authorizes technical development becomes increasingly obscured, embedded deep within social and technological systems, such that responsibility for making decisions becomes increasingly difficult to identify. Winner alerts us to the political complexity of technology that means when things go wrong, it is difficult to blame either the materiality of the technology or even the individual who invented or 'created' new things. Technology only *appears* to be 'autonomous' or a determinative historical force; in fact, it is impossible to separate it from economic, social and political forces.

If Winner identifies the political complexity of modern technological systems, Stephen Hill (1988) picks up the slightly different theme of their cultural embeddedness. He argues that the symbolic significance of technological artefacts depends on a negotiation between the life-world in which they are used and the cultural context of world-views that surrounds them (Hill 1988: 46). This perspective gives Hill a way of analysing the impact of technologies that are imported into cultures in which they were not developed. If in the receiving culture the 'alignment' between technology and culture is poor, there can be damaging effects, sometimes for the technology (as with the Cook Islanders who buried their pick-up truck after a year, Hill 1988: 112), and sometimes for the culture (the transformation of traditional fishing techniques in Sri Lanka through the introduction of mechanized boats and nylon fishing lines, Hill 1988: 76–8). Hill's critique is focused more on cultural imperialism than on the relationship between technology and society but it does allow him to make the point that technology, and particularly technological artefacts, are always dependent on other cultural resources. These are first of all, knowledge (of how an internal combustion engine works) and, second, a technological infrastructure (the network of spare part suppliers). Together knowledge and infrastructure constitute a 'technological frame' (Hill 1988: 160) that makes its own demands on society for resources and cultural change. This theme not only echoes Winner's 'technological systems' but also the impact of 'technique' in Ellul and 'technological rationality' in Marcuse. There is a difference, however, in that other critics are keen to emphasize the integration of technological thinking within the culture whereas Hill treats it as a distinct 'text' which is just one of a number in modern cultures so that the 'tragedy' of technology is 'the submission of human purpose to the external systematic ordering of human affairs by the industrialised technological frame' (Hill 1988: 230).

Hill's solution is a political ideological one:

once accepted into industrial society, the cultural values of the technology text have had power to command the human constitution of cultural meanings into alignment with the central values of the text itself. The task of reshaping the culture–technology nexus is to break this alignment at the gateways where the values of the technology text have entered wider culture, and to reassert a culture of 'autonomy' within everyday life.

(Hill 1988: 240)

But this seems to ignore the embeddedness of technology in the everyday lives of people; it is not an abstract belief system but a set of lived, practical arrangements. The 'culture–technology nexus' is a set of technologies that have been taken up and incorporated; everyday life cannot be autonomous from technology since it is part of it.

The themes of technology as culture and technology as politics are conjoined in Andrew Feenberg's (1999; 2002) writing on technology. Rather like Hill's 'technology text', he refers to a 'technical code' to describe the conjunction of technological innovations with social interest as, for example, the assembly line which blends technology and culture to achieve both functional effects in terms of production and social power in the form of control over workers. His argument is that the inventions and discoveries of technology are things that really work in themselves and are socially neutral but when they are taken up in a social context, they are shaped and joined together in particular configurations that reflect the interests of those holding power.[8] He suggests that technology might be available for capitalism to sustain its hegemony but it might also be available as a resource that could be adopted for socialist ideals. Feenberg's critical perspective on technology argues that it is not necessarily an anti-human or anti-society force and as an example he anticipates Negri and Hardt's analysis in *Empire* (1999) by arguing that computer technology is not only useful for control but also for communication and 'any technology that enhances human contact has democratic potentialities' (2002: 92).

But here we have the problem that Marcuse calls 'harmonization' where technology can appear to be both good and bad and its development seems to respond to the politico-cultural tensions that surround it. The motor car is not only a commodity whose technological development has been driven by the desire of capitalist enterprise to exploit markets. It is a useful, liberating device that has become safer, more reliable, longer-lasting and uses scarce resources ever more efficiently. There is considerable debate about the way that hegemonic interests have shaped the emergence of the petrol car over the electric car (see, for example, Schiffer 2000 who argues that it is the gendered behaviour of the majority of purchasers that was important in the gasoline car becoming dominant in the middle-class market). But there is also a debate about new forms of 'zero-emission' cars. Manufacturers have responded to critics of petrol technology by producing a range of hybrid electric vehicles which seem likely to challenge the dominance of petrol engine cars in the next few decades (Motavalli 2000: 108). Where Marcuse sees a process of steady incorporation within the hegemony of technological rationality, Feenberg sees a dialectical relation in which the political effects of cultural tensions feed into technological development. However, Feenberg does make an interesting move in distinguishing two levels of technology: 'primary instrumentalization' is about *'functional constitution'* which involves 'reifying' natural objects and transforming them to serve a use, and 'secondary instrumentalization', which is to do with the *'realization* of the constituted objects and subjects in actual networks and devices' (1999: 202). Primary instrumentalization involves 'decontextualization, calculation and control' – the sorts of processes that we normally associate with the application of technological rationality to bring new technologies into being. Secondary instrumentalization, however, is the more practical level of incorporating new technologies into the material life of a society. It is at this secondary level that political intervention can affect how technologies are incorporated within a society and the 'reverse adaptation' can be resisted. Once technologies have been formed in the primary process, they cannot be undone but how they are modified for later use is something that is not determined by technological imperative.

In Gilbert Simondon's concept of 'concretization', of how new technology becomes everyday stuff, he suggests that technological innovations have to adapt to demands that may be disconnected or even incompatible. Feenberg gives the example of the house that gets its heat from the sun rather than from burning fossil fuels so that the need for heat and light as well as environmental constraints are built into the design (1999: 217). Concretization does not follow a simple logic of technological rationality but reflexively responds to adapt function to the context of use, thereby shaping technologies to their social and natural environment – the inverse of Winner's 'reverse adaptation'. The difficulty with Feenberg's argument is that it does rather sound like modern capitalism doing good business. Because there is an increasing ideological commitment to the environment among customers – no small matter as Feenberg would no doubt point out – then house builders will begin to make new houses more 'environmentally friendly'. But prior to this ideological shift, capitalist enterprises have long since recognized that there are a variety of ways of appealing to consumers so that multiplying function has become a standard strategy of technological development. Cavity walls, double glazing, loft insulation, thermal building blocks are all, in the UK, subject to building regulation standards that periodically change to improve the conservation of heat and so energy. Consumers, however, appreciate these effects both in terms of lower fuel bills and having an easier house to heat and keep warm; the process of concretization seems to be well integrated within capitalist societies. Mobile phone technology was initially driven by the idea of separating the functionality of the telephone from a location fixed through wired connections. But along the way other related technologies have been integrated (SMS, WAP, imaging, games, clocks, and so on) to increase functionality within the device with a response from customers that has varied over time. Now the integration of other technologies is not driven simply by customer demand but by technological exigency; the overlap between cell-based pager technology and cell phone technology, the potential for data transfer between computer systems by telephone, the digitization of images as mere data, the development of liquid crystal displays for a number of different purposes. In other words, new functionality arises out of any context as an idea that is possible and is then tried out on actual customers where it may be successful (SMS) or not (WAP) according to how it is integrated into the context of useage.

Feenberg's concept of secondary instrumentalization does point to the complexity of how technologies are taken up and integrated into our everyday lives and how this has an impact on how, and even whether, the technology is successful. This is a useful counter to the tendency amongst critics of technology to imply that an imperative logic links the materiality of technology to its social networks. Feenberg also hints at how a political resistance to technology does not need to operate at the level of planning and design but can have significant effects at the level of consumption, adoption and usage. This does provide an opportunity, for example, to argue that sustainable technology should be integrated into the everyday material practice of a society even while the technological systems lag behind the recognition of its importance. Feenberg proposes a strategy of 'democratic rationalization' to 'signify user interventions that challenge undemocratic power structures rooted in modern technology' (1999: 108).

Conclusion

The emphasis in this chapter has been on drawing out the themes of the major critics of technology who have seen it as not only changing material civilization but also as changing the relationship between material life and social life during the twentieth century. There is in the critiques of Mumford, Heidegger, Marcuse and Ellul a concern that a new form of materialism, introduced as technology which binds humans to objects in new ways, has changed the course of history. While the basic thrust of their arguments is for the reassertion of immaterial human values – those of the human spirit, of imagination, of spontaneity, of aesthetics and of emotion – they often overlook the way that these are inseparable from the material lives of human beings and of society. Their warnings were appropriate and it is not too late to resist arguments that claim a technological imperative, the 'must have' of technologies that will have enormous material benefits (those in favour of genetic engineering spring to mind) but which involve the creation of a standing-reserve of forces that are beyond our imagination.

The later critics of technology have responded to these themes to point out the political and cultural features of technological systems, re-emphasizing the interrelationship between technology and society, re-articulating the continuity between materiality and sociality. There remains an argument that has not been persuasively rebutted and that is the Marcusian political interpretation of Heidegger's 'danger'. Industrialization has brought a mode of technological thinking that when allied with social forces strengthened by that thinking, is remarkably resilient to resistance, threatening the spiritual and material freedom of humankind as it adapts and responds to complaints and disagreements:

> Hatred and frustration are deprived of their specific target, and the technical veil conceals the reproduction of inequality and enslavement. With technical progress as its instrument, unfreedom – in the sense of man's subjection to his productive apparatus – is perpetuated and intensified in the form of many liberties and comforts.
>
> (Marcuse 1991: 35)

Although the critics of technology have given us salient pointers to the cultural dynamics of technology, advising that things are more complex than they at first appear and that history is not already written within the trajectory of technological innovation, they have avoided dealing with the practical and detailed ways that materiality is being altered in technological societies. Before moving towards the embodied nature of being with materiality and attempting to develop the beginnings of a method of analysing material interaction, in the next chapter I will turn to look at the relationship between material agency and human agency. One of the characteristics of technology that its critics have recognized is that it is not a 'thing', not an entity with an internal logic that determines its progress but a merging of material and social components that produce patterns of action that are both material and social. What happens then, when we begin to distinguish between the agency of people and the agency of things?

4   Agency, affordance and actor-networks

Introduction

The debate about the relationship between technology and society discussed in Chapter 3 treats technology as a process which we found to be entangled with the processes of society. What that debate tends to overlook are the more practical relationships between people and things as individual beings which mediate culture and sociality. In this chapter I want to begin to explore some ideas about how material objects are constituted in relation to individual people. From the perspective of the individual, objects are incorporated into the life of a person and extend his or her being in the world, both the material world and the social world. Looked at from the perspective of society, the object is a vehicle of the intentions and designs of the culture that can shape the actions of the individual. The various approaches I will explore suggest that material things have some measure of 'agency'. To be sure, they have never, at least as yet, been able to demonstrate sufficient autonomous intention or reflective awareness to be equivalent to human agency. Instead objects acquire agency from the human actions which form them, including those actions which take them up into use; the agency of objects is essentially human agency transferred to material objects. The term 'agency' refers to the power to do or to act and, conveniently, the word also refers to the power to act on the part of another. My telephone answering machine operates as my agent, responding on my behalf to calls intended for me. To act in this role it must identify itself as being my agent (through the message it gives callers) and accurately record messages for me to deal with later. Its actions stand in my stead and yet no one is under the illusion that it is me (except those who start to respond immediately when they hear my voice and then feel irritated and cheated when they realize it is just a machine). Although I might claim the answering machine as my agent, it is also the agent of the culture through which it acquired its specific characteristics of design and manufacture and through the material context in which I use it, that is to say, a telephone network of companies, exchanges, lines and codes.

Marshall McLuhan was fascinated by the way that technology merged with human society to extend the power of people to act in their world, both communicatively and physically:

> To extend our bodily postures and motions into new materials, by way of amplification, is a constant drive for more power. Most of our bodily stresses are interpreted as needs for extending storage and mobility functions, such as occur, also in speech, money and writing. All manner of utensils are a yielding to this bodily stress by means of extensions of the body.
>
> (McLuhan 1994: 181)

For McLuhan what was significant about the motor car as an extension of the human body was not its signifying power of sexual or social status but its power as a 'hot, explosive medium' of social communication that could move people about much more quickly than the pedestrian's legs or the rider's horse (1994: 221). McLuhan saw the impact of technology in its creation of objects that extended the embodied agency of individual humans rather than becoming objects in themselves acting on behalf or in concert with human agents. But the human activity of moving about their physical and social environment was extended by the power of the car in a way that revised existing social boundaries of class and status, changing the shape of modern societies both geographically and culturally. As Horkheimer reminds us, 'the proposition that tools are prolongations of human organs can be inverted to state that the organs are also prolongations of the tools' (1999: 201).

In this chapter we will see how human agency is invested in material objects through emotion, through meaning, through perception and through interconnection. Sometimes the agency seems to be autonomous, as in the artwork or the telephone answering machine, so that the object acts independently of the human on whose behalf it works. In the language that Alfred Gell develops, the agency of the object operates as an 'index', pointing back to its human origins while apparently remote from them. At other times the agency of an object is tied to its contact with a human so that for Serge Tisseron, the emotions invested in the object are released as it is incorporated into human actions. For James Gibson, the agency of the object is discovered in perception as what the object 'affords' or offers to the human who comes into contact with it. And for Bruno Latour, Michelle Callon and their colleagues, the agency of the object lies in how it assists or resists the networked actions of a series of actors including other objects.

Affect and agency

One of the features of late modernity is that a myriad of material objects are created and used as tools; if we ever stop to think about them, we regard them as 'mere' objects that do not in anyway compete with humans for status as beings. Objects are there for us to use and dispose of in whatever way we wish; we may treat them well or badly without any concern for their rights or feelings because they have none. Just as people in other civilizations treated slaves or animals with little or no concern for their welfare, so we treat objects as possessions, chattels over which we have complete dominion. But when we are not thinking about it 'rationally', we do sometimes ascribe human characteristics to objects, just as we do to animals. This is not quite the same thing as treating them as within the category of human beings because if we are confronted with a choice or decision, we will distinguish the human from the object (and those who do not are regarded as rather odd). I swear at my computer accusing it of wilfulness when it malfunctions although I'm slightly uncomfortable that I'm swearing at the material object of the box of electronics rather than the software which is the usual cause of the problem but which is too intangible to see as a 'thing' with agency. I knew a Cambridge don who, it was whispered, had burst into inconsolable tears when an irreplaceable bottle of vintage brandy slipped from his hands and smashed on the floor. We can become deeply attached to heirlooms or personal objects that we imbue with something of the character of a person, or a place or an experience. Such objects transcend the status of 'mere' objects as we seem to love or hate them, expressing emotions of tenderness or loathing through words or gestures that we normally reserve for animate beings.

The French psychoanalyst, Serge Tisseron (1999) has identified a number of aspects of emotional and practical relationships with material objects through which they begin to take on something of the status of human agents. Rather than simply seeing things as extensions of human beings, as Marshall McLuhan seems to, he argues that the prosthetic quality of objects is balanced by their 'introjection' or 'inclusion' within the psychic states of those whose bodies they extend (1999: 133). As he writes about clothes, monuments, art objects and the artefacts of our everyday lives, Tisseron points out how individual contact with things is not merely functional or simply symbolic but is also, at the same time, linked to our individual identity and sense of self. One of the psychological theories that he draws on is Winnicott's concept of the 'transitional object' – Tisseron uses the example of Linus, a character in the *Peanuts* cartoon strip, who carries about a piece of blanket – that is treated as a replacement for the mother figure (1999: 37). The 'transitional object' for the adult becomes much more flexible and is manipulated for more complex purposes than simply providing a sense of emotional security. Nonetheless, the intimate relationship with the feel of a material, its smell, familiarity and the sense of protection from the world beyond the self it brings, remains an aspect of the way that we wear our clothes. Tisseron writes of the difference between the outer clothes that present a social face projecting signs that the individual feels comfortable with, while underclothes are more to do with intimacy and the sense of self that needs to be protected:

> One can, for example, wear black undergarments and coloured clothes, or the reverse. In the same way, silky materials can be arranged between the body and the rough materials directed outwards, or the opposite. In the end, the volume of outer fabrics can overlay clothes tightly like a secret wrapping. The dynamic of the outer garments – more 'sociable' – and of the undergarments – more 'intimate' – tells of the emotional and affective state of everyone at every moment.
>
> (Tisseron 1999: 46)[1]

The way that material objects provide a bridge between the inner psychic life of the individual and the outer social life of the world around is not fixed but varies and may involve contradictory or reversible meanings. In writing about everyday domestic objects, Tisseron argues that meanings are not fixed or stable but are managed by the individual to meet both the demands of the situation and their emotional state. He refers to Bourdieu's concept of 'habitus' as he recognizes that relationships with objects often originate in the common practices acquired from the society around us. Nonetheless, objects can carry emotional and personal meanings so that plates, bought by one's mother, are brought out when friends come to dinner, making links between the inheritance of emotional and practical ways of being and the building of present relationships (Tisseron 1999: 78). Each piece of domestic equipment is associated with memories – some banal, some of deep significance – and is tied up with the personal history of those who use them (see Dant 2000b). They are vehicles for carrying the individual's past and for enabling him or her to realize emotional as well as practical relationships, with the self and with others. As he accepts Bourdieu's account of the habitus as a social origin of the practices, language and the significances of material life, Tisseron points out that the individual does not draw on a single habitus, and their behaviour is not determined in any mechanical sense. He recognizes that Bourdieu's concept is about dispositions but prefers the account of Bernard Lahire (1998) who suggests that the social actor calls on 'schemes of action' appropriate to the situation. These schemes of action are not simply habits but ways of seeing, feeling, speaking and making do, schemes of perception and understanding, that are based on past experiences but are applied, not necessarily consciously, anew to each situation (Tisseron 1999: 143).

What material objects do for people then is not simply symbolic, not simply a presentation of signs, but is tangled up with the practical arrangements that the person lives out through the activities of their body. Such bodily motor actions in the material world have an emotional quality at the same time as carrying social meanings as signs. Tisseron expresses this in a complex idea that combines the senses with emotions and motor actions of the body: 'The specific form of symbolization put into play in clothing is from the first sensory-affective-motor' (1999: 43).[2] Material objects act as a conduit that extends the agency of the body and the person into the world while also providing a channel from the world back into the person. Things are agents of the self but also of the society towards the individual so that he refers to them as 'reversible' in the sense that they carry memories, signs, social relationships to the person but can then be used by the person to express and manage personality and an emotional life. In a simple way this is achieved by the actions which direct objects away from the person – giving them as a gift, selling them, putting them away or hiding them. But the way that objects are used can be more complex and more intimately tied to the emotional life.

Objects used as tools can act as extensions of the body but they also direct sensory information into the body so that they can become as part of it (Tisseron 1999: 147). The American psychologist of bodily sensory apparatus, James Gibson, also recognizes that while the proprioceptive senses within muscles and joints distinguish what is in and what is outside of the body, the visual systems of the body can deal with objects as if they are part of the body:

This is what happens when a tool is used in place of the hand itself for manipulating an object, as when grasping it with pliers instead of with the fingers, or striking it with a hammer instead of the fist. The felt action of muscles, joints, and skin is then rather different, but the visible action is essentially the same and the visual system can easily control the motor output. The situation is similar when one uses the steering-wheel of a vehicle instead of one's legs to guide the direction of one's locomotion.

(Gibson 1968: 36)

But Tisseron goes rather further to suggest that the psychic life of the person is transferred to objects through which emotions are expressed and made manifest. There is, for example, a pleasure in what he calls, following Ives Hendrick, an 'instinct of mastery', when a person enjoys learning to use something and then enjoys using it with skill (Tisseron 1999: 135). People who successfully learn to drive will experience this sort of pleasure which is about control over the object as a way of being in the world rather than a sensual pleasure. The bodily engagements with objects may also extend actions which might have been made within or against the body such as wringing one's hands or rubbing one's skin. Such actions can both dissipate and display emotion and a similar effect may be achieved, for example, by cleaning the car ('Some men seem, moreover, to spend more of their time occupied with the bodywork that covers their car than with the skin that covers their body',[3] Tisseron 1999: 150). So cleaning the car may be at the same time a way of externalizing emotions, both releasing and dealing with psychic tension. Using objects that make a noise such as a car or a vacuum cleaner may also work to both express and absorb anger or anguish. Tisseron suggests that tending or repairing objects or on the other hand dealing with them roughly or throwing them away, are also ways of externalizing emotions that might otherwise either be suppressed or work back on the body. The material relation between the human being and the objects around him or her enables feelings and emotions to be pushed from inside to out, from the psyche to the surface of the body and then beyond through things. This psychoanalytic perspective on mundane relationships with everyday objects goes further than incorporating them within rituals that have social effects, as for example McCracken does (1988: 84–8, see also Chapter 2 above), by recognizing that the agency of persons spills out from their body into the objects with which their body deals.

In emphasizing the emotional engagement with objects, Tisseron significantly modifies the idea, so characteristic of the sociological literature on consumption, that they are simply signs. He argues that it is not only through quasi-linguistic symbolizations that objects mediate between the individual and the society that he or she lives in, but that it is through gesture, such as the making or choosing of objects and the way they are taken up in techniques and practices, that mediations are maintained and achieved. As mediators between individuals and their society, objects become involved in actions which are at the same time of symbolic and psychological significance. This process of mediation is different from the view of symbolic communication, characteristic of analysing mass media, in which meaning is separated from the act in which it is produced. What Tisseron argues is that every act of exteriorization is also an act of interiorization, symbolization in the material world is both social and psychic, collective and personal (1999: 180–3). And in understanding the place of material objects in a social world we must recognize that 'Objects are not only extensions of our motor or sensory organs. They are, more fundamentally, extensions of our mind' (1999: 217).[4]

Art and agency

Tisseron incorporates screens, art and visual objects in his discussion of how things mediate individual emotion and cultural understandings.

However, the agency that he ascribes to objects emphasizes their capacity as a vehicle for the feelings of particular individuals. When he discusses memorials and art objects he describes how they carry shared understandings and values but does not focus on the mechanics of this process. In quite a different way, before his untimely death, the anthropologist Alfred Gell set out a remarkable way of thinking about material objects, specifically art objects, as 'the equivalent of persons, or more precisely, social agents' (1998: 7). His interest was in setting up an anthropological theory of art that did not presuppose the nature of the art object either in terms of aesthetics or in terms of institutional structures that might identify it as 'art'. Instead he developed a theory of the agency of objects in which the art object could be a specific instance. Rather than being constrained by a philosophical account of agency that would require that membership of the category be consistent and stable, he argued that 'things' could be treated as agents simply because that is how human beings from time to time treated them. It is in attributing agency to objects, such as a little girl treating her doll as if it had will and intention, that for social purposes objects can be deemed to have agency. He points out that the admiration accorded to Michaelangelo's statue of David is on occasion equivalent to the primacy with which a child treats her doll's importance as a being in the world. But it is through the mundane example of human relationships with cars in contemporary culture that he makes the idea of things as social agents ring true:

> A car, just as a possession and a means of transport is not intrinsically a locus of agency, either the owner's agency or its own. But it is in fact very difficult for a car owner not to regard a car as a body-part, a prosthesis, something invested with his (or her) own social agency vis-à-vis other social agents. Just as a salesman confronts a potential client with his body (his good teeth and well-brushed hair, bodily indexes of business competence) so he confronts the buyer with his car (a Mondeo, late registration, black) another, detachable, part of his body available for inspection and approval. Conversely, an injury suffered by the car is a personal blow, an outrage, even though the damage can be made good and the insurance company will pay. Not only is the car a locus of the owner's agency, and a conduit through which the agency of others (bad drivers, vandals) may affect him – it is also the locus of an 'autonomous' agency of its own.
>
> (Gell 1998: 18)

The car as prosthesis or bodily extension seems to constitute its agency merely as an extension of its owner. But Gell is serious when he argues that its agency is also autonomous. He describes his own Toyota – known to the family as 'Tollyolly', 'Olly' for short – as a thing that he 'esteems', that is 'considerate' but if it were to break down in the middle of the night, far from home, he would regard this as 'an act of gross treachery' for which he would hold the car 'personally and morally culpable' (Gell 1998: 18–19).

What Gell is doing is to point out that while it may not be adequate for philosophical purposes, for anthropological purposes, people do, from time to time, treat things as persons. This does not mean that the object always has the capacity of agency for all actors at all times, so that he sometimes treats his car as an autonomous agent but in general he is perfectly aware that it is a thing and as such has no mind, no intention and no will. Gell points out that human agency is exercised in the material world and mind, intention or will are only evidenced by some causal, material event in that world. This, he argues, means that 'it is not paradoxical to understand agency as a factor of the ambience as a whole, a global characteristic of the world of people and things in which we live, rather than as an attribute of the human psyche, exclusively' (Gell 1998: 20). The more effective that objects are in being implicated in material, causal events in the world, the more we are likely to attribute agency to them. This means that objects like cars and other mechanical or semi-autonomous objects (such as computers running programs) are more likely to be treated as having agency than simple inanimate objects whose causal role is easily identified. The 'black-box' effect, where the precise workings of an object are not known or understood by those using it, promotes a tendency to suspect that there is a 'ghost in the machine'. However, Gell modulates his claim about the attribution of agency by distinguishing between 'primary' agents who are intentional beings and 'secondary' agents which are 'artefacts, dolls, cars, works of art etc. through which primary agents distribute their agency in the causal milieu, and thus render their agency effective' (1998: 20). As secondary agents, objects may lack intention but they do have causal efficacy; what is ambiguous is where the intention that leads to the materiality of causal efficacy actually lies. The breakdown of a car may originate with poor servicing, design or manufacture of parts or even with poor driving technique ('riding' the clutch, 'caning' the gearbox, etc.). It also may arise simply because components are worn out having reached the end of their life as material entities. Identifying causal agency in such situations is often difficult, even impossible, and may make little difference to future actions (e.g. getting the car repaired).

In thinking through the agency of art and other artefacts, Gell refers to them as 'indexes', invoking Peirce's semiology where the object is a causal or material sign rather than a signifier in a quasi-linguistic system. Smoke is treated as an index of fire because that is what usually causes it, rather than because of a social convention such as that which links a linguistic sign to its material referent. The index falls somewhere between the 'law of nature' of a physical cause and the 'social convention' of an agreed meaning to refer to what seems to be the case in the material world. The artefact is then an 'index' of its origins, pointing to its maker and his or her intentions, and to the culture it is inserted into. If the maker is forgotten, as with the Kula shells in Melanesia, their originator is treated as the person who is giving them away. The object also indexes the recipient, audience or the person for whom the object is intended: 'A Ferrari sports car, parked in the street, indexes the class-fraction of "millionaire playboys" for whom such cars are made. It also indexes the general public who can only admire such vehicles and envy their owners' (Gell 1998: 24). When the index is an art object that represents something, its capacity as an index is through some actual resemblance to that which it represents which stimulates an inference or interpretation.

Gell's theory was designed to show that artworks could be meaningful to people from completely different cultures and from different times if they were understood as social agents that referred to their makers, to their representational origins in the world and to the audiences to whom they were directed. He uses the theory to analyse the social relations around what he called the 'art nexus' which is too specific for my discussion of the social significance of materiality and agency. However, one theme that emerges as he applies his theory to specific empirical instances which does, I think, have general applicability, is that of the 'distributed person'. There is a common-sense idea of human agency as residing in the discreet self, bounded by the materiality of the body and its incorporated mind. This is perhaps a product of the increasing individualism, combined with the loss of a sense of religious continuity between people, that has characterized the trajectory of modernity. Instead of seeing our destinies as the result either of fate or God's will, modernity has come to be characterized by increased emphasis on the construction of our own individual futures through a 'reflexive project of the self' (Giddens 1991). However, Gell explores the artistic productions of various ancient cultures and shows that agency ascribed to gods and other superhuman forces is also taken to inhabit material objects and that the agency is distributed through them. From one direction, he is suggesting that agency is not originally human but emerges from the religious beliefs of a social group. From another direction, he suggests that the agency of a human individual can be distributed through a series of objects. I will briefly explore these two dimensions of distributed person-hood as ways in which agency can exist within material objects – both in ancient cultures and modern ones.

The first form is in effect idolatory in which material objects, shaped by humans, are treated as having an agency which acts in the world. Magic, for example, eschews scientific notions of cause and effect in the material world because, argues Gell, it depends on a form of causation in which *intentions cause events to happen in the vicinity of agents*' (1998: 101). That is to say, rather than see all causation as having to originate in physical forces, magic sees the world of material causation as arising in human intentions that are expressed and given material form in acts of magic. What is important is the intense expression of intention that in the case of 'volt sorcery' involves an image of the victim, often made of wax, that is subjected to injury or destruction with the result that the victim of the sorcery suffers the same injuries. The person-hood of the victim is extended or distributed into their material representations through which they become vulnerable to material injury. Gell points out that this process is not restricted to 'superstitious beliefs' but also occurs, for example, in a contemporary photograph of a person that is subjected to ridicule or caricature; 'as social persons, we are present, not just in our singular bodies, but in everything in our surroundings which bears witness to our existence, our attributes and our agency' (1998: 103). Letting down someone's tyres or posting dogshit through their door is not just practically unpleasant but does damage to their distributed person-hood.

Gell's examples are predominantly from the anthropological literature on Tahitian, Maori and other traditional cultures but he points out that the buildings erected by western religions are also material manifestations of God's power and agency. They are of course also manifestations of human agency in which there is an exchange of status and power around the idolatry of His agency. Ordinary people may treat the idea that God resides in material forms with some suspicion and they are likely to have little difficulty in distinguishing between the image or object and what it represents. Nonetheless, Gell points out, referring back to the remarks about his car, anthropomorphism or animism is not restricted to those who are confused about the nature of the material world. That idols are not treated as 'alive' is attested to by the fact that when they show life – when the plaster saint cries or bleeds – it is treated as a miracle, something quite beyond the normal process of idol worship. When people believe that a material object, such as a cathedral, carries some degree of social agency, it is not because they believe that it is biologically alive and it is not important how alike it is to living beings (Gell 1998: 125).

The second form of distributed person-hood that Gell describes is at first sight rather more restricted. He argues that the individual can be seen as embodied in their material products such as the *œuvre* of an artist; different works refer to each other across time as if they were extensions of the artist's mind. Using Marcel Duchamp's *œuvre* Gell argues elegantly that earlier works prefigure later works – he uses Husserl's language of objects that 'protend' future ones – and later works refer back to earlier works as a retention of ideas and forms. Gell's account of Duchamp and his use of Husserl's and Bergson's conceptions of time to explore how agency is distributed over time into the material world is both fascinating and illuminating. But his major point is fairly straightforward – human transformation of the material world occurs both in biographical time and historical time, both expressing the individual and tying that individual to the cultural world in which they live. This distribution of person-hood is recoverable by others at some other point in time – exactly as Gell does with Duchamp. The expression of intentionality in any single creative act both builds on and refers to previous creative acts and refers and responds to the socio-material world around it. As Gell points out, this also happens in a rather more mundane way with contemporary house extensions where the owner's intentions are realized in a material form that overlays the intentions both of the original builder and previous owners. As we distribute our person-hood in the material world in this sort of way, mixing it with those of others, nothing is simply determined: 'What gets built is whatever seems the best possible compromise in the light of all the practical difficulties and constraints entering into the situation; given that the decision to build "something or other" has already been taken' (Gell 1998: 257).

Affordances

Alfred Gell's account of the agency of material objects situates them in the material culture in which they originate and survive and, unlike Tisseron's, does not depend on particular lines of emotion and affect so much as cultural practices and attitudes that establish and sustain that agency. A version of the agency of material objects that attempts to avoid either emotional or cultural lines of connection with the social world is James Gibson's notion of 'affordances'. Gibson is a psychologist of the senses who, without reducing sensory awareness to neurophysiology, grounds his account in the biological possibilities of the human sensory apparatus. In this account, the agency of humans does not imbue the material objects around them, nor does ritual distribute human agency among the things of the world. Human agency is solidly located in the physiology of the human animal that includes a sensory apparatus not quite like any other animal. One aspect of this sensory apparatus is the human capacity for cognition but this is relatively downplayed in Gibson's psychology, operating as an aspect of the functioning of the senses rather than as their centre of direction as in a full-blown cognitive psychology.

Gibson tries to understand how the human orients itself to the material world in which it lives through the retinal image received in human vision. He is particularly interested in how the senses operate when the human is moving and how sensory information is organized to allow the human animal to proceed with confidence. Once moving at any speed, in, say, a car, the human perception, judgement and decision-making of the driver operates more or less unconsciously, responding to the environment more quickly than conscious cognition can calculate (Gibson 1982: 130, fn10). The horse will add its own intentionality to that of its rider to avoid

obstacles or take opportunities; the car driver only has the mechanical prosthetic of the car to help. And yet, remarkably, most humans, given adequate
eyesight and controls that they can manipulate, are able to learn to drive
competently at speeds in excess of 30 miles an hour on roads full of obstacles including other moving vehicles. Writing in 1938 about this impressive
extension of ordinary human agency through a material object that he calls
a 'locomotion tool', Gibson proposed that the driver perceives a 'field of
safe travel' where the car can go unimpeded (1982: 120). Bounding or
intruding into the 'positive valence' of this safe field are 'negative valences'
or obstacles such as the kerb, parked cars and moving traffic. Within the
field are the invisible boundaries of the 'minimum stopping zone' and the
'halo of avoidance' around obstacles that are brought to perception by the
driver's experience (Gibson 1982: 127). As Gibson presents this account
with line drawings of the road situation in plan format, these perceptual
categories appear as fixed material properties of the driver's car. In fact, of
course, they are properties of the driver who has acquired them through
learning about what works and what is culturally acceptable. The field
would vary according to the speed of the car and the driver's experience –
learner drivers progressively learn to 'read' the road ahead, some drivers will
confidently pass closer to obstacles than others. The driver will take into
account the material properties of the vehicle they are driving and modu-
late their attention to the field ahead according to the type of road, taking
into account the sorts of obstacles or dangers that it holds (Laurier 2004).
The road itself is a cultural as well as material construction with its regulations, directions and signified injunctions that will shape the perceived
'field of safe travel' (see Horkheimer 1947: 98; Marcuse 1998: 46).

    Gibson's early account of how visual perception works in relation to
driving is rather fixed and mechanical, taking little account of human variability or cultural impact and only recognizing in passing that other
sensory channels – kinaesthetic, tactile and auditory – are involved (1982:
134). In his later work (Gibson 1979), he exchanges the concept of 'valence'
for 'affordance' to refer to the perceived characteristics of material objects.
Rather than simply a negative or positive value being perceived in the
object, it is imbued with a set of properties and propensities which are
apparent to a perceiver. This more closely approaches a notion of agency in
which the object and human being interact than was found in his earlier
writing. As he rethinks the way that vision works, Gibson puts the emphasis
on the material environment rather than on what happens within the
body. This is not the material world of physics in which precise weights,
vectors and forces might be specified but the environment as it is perceived
by an animal, specifically a human animal, as it inhabits and moves
through it. Instead of regarding the eye and brain as the locus of vision, he
begins to think of it as a whole system, an 'ambient optic array', that
includes the head, the body and the ground which supports it. In other

words, what we see is not just what is at the centre of our sight when we fix on a point, it includes the background and what is in our peripheral vision. This shift in perspective recognizes that the operation of vision occurs in response to the environment so that what happens physiologically in vision cannot be treated abstractly as a mechanism outside of the situation in which it occurs. Think of the driver of the car again; he or she can see all sorts of things in their peripheral vision that do not attract their attention and as the eyes and head move to focus on specific things the field of vision is continually changed and extended. This development of Gibson's understanding of perception moves from a physiological psychology towards the phenomenological approach to embodiment that I will discuss in the next chapter.

All the body's senses orient the animal to its environment but it is sight which is most important in establishing the relationship between the material body of the animal and the materiality of the environment. It is because the body, or at least the eyes or the head, move while the ambient optic array remains more or less static that we can make judgements about speed and distance, for example. For Gibson, the environment is made up of a medium (air or water), substances and surfaces that have properties to which the body's senses can respond. Light bounces off surfaces, travels through the medium and is received by our eyes and sound emanates and reverberates to be received by our ears. These properties of the material environment are, for Gibson, not a set of physical properties to be described and specified – although they are quite consistent with such a physical account – they are 'affordances': 'All these offerings of nature, these possibilities and opportunities, these *affordances* as I will call them are invariant. They have been strikingly constant throughout the whole evolution of animal life' (Gibson 1979: 18). If the senses are the way that the material world is present for a human person, then this is also how they apprehend their own body. Gibson argues that all the senses are to some extent 'propriosensitive' as well as 'exterosensitive' (1979: 115). I can see my hand, watch my feet in peripheral vision as I walk, smell the emanations of my body, hear the sound of my own voice and, through what are usually treated as the proprioceptors, feel the position of my limbs and body through sensors in my muscles and joints. As Gibson points out, the senses work together so that the information from the different senses is not processed separately or distinctly, including the sense of our own bodies. This view of sensory perception deviated from the traditional psycho-physiology at the time Gibson was writing but it accords well with Merleau-Ponty's phenomenology, as we shall see in Chapter 5.

Although the word 'afford' is familiar, Gibson coins the neologism 'affordance' to point to the way in which an animal perceives the values and meanings of things in the environment simultaneously with perceiving them as things. He says that affordance refers to the 'complementarity of the animal and environment' in which it is the physical properties of a material entity that offer something to the animal (1979: 127). His concept then refers to the physicality of the material world in relation to specific animals rather than being an attempt to *objectively* or abstractly account for its physicality in terms of measurement and scales. The materiality of the world offers possibilities to the particular materiality of an animal so a kitchen chair will afford me the possibility of sitting down, resting my trunk with my legs still supporting their weight, but for my cat it affords the possibility of sitting down while supporting its whole body. The idea of affordance neatly avoids the tricky idea of 'function' in which we become concerned with the specific intention behind an object's design and manufacture.

Gibson suggests that the origin of the concept of affordance lies in Kurt Lewin's term *Aufforderungscharakter* which has been variously translated as the 'invitation character' or the 'valence' of an object (Gibson 1979: 138; Marrow 1969: 56). There is a sense of direction, of the valence having a vector of attraction or repulsion, that is phenomenological rather than physical in Gibson's taking up of this term.[5] This chimes with George Mead's remarks that certain objects 'call out' to human beings to be used in a certain way (1962: 278–80).[6] However, what an object 'invites' or 'offers' is then a blend of the physical and cultural; the physical properties of an object, be it a hill or a hammer, fit in with physical properties of human bodies (or most human bodies) but the sorts of things they invite are culturally specified. This would be accepted by Mead but Gibson is a psychologist, keen to delimit the way that material objects can be used in terms of the material relation of bodies and the world. As a result, he does not recognize culture and its variability or the constraints it creates but treats affordances as fixed properties of things:

> The affordance of something does *not change* as the need of the observer changes. The observer may or may not perceive or attend to the affordance, according to his needs, but the affordance, being invariant, is always there to be perceived. An affordance is not bestowed on an object by a need of an observer and his act of perceiving it. The object offers what it does because it is what it is. To be sure we define *what it is* in terms of ecological physics instead of physical physics, and it therefore possesses meaning and value to begin with. But this is meaning and value of a new sort.
>
> (Gibson 1979: 138–9)

This asserted immutability of affordances depends on the presumed stability of the material world that is not shared by the social world. In fact, the social world generates new ways of forming objects that may look different but lend themselves to old uses or look much the same and lend themselves to new uses. The change in the material life of human societies that in Chapter 2 I called 'material civilization' means that there are always newly emerging contexts in which the affordance of existing objects is continually revised. But even within a moment of history material objects are taken into human action in a variety of ways that is constrained but not determined by its physical properties. I can stand on my chair to change a light bulb, I can jam it under a doorknob to act as a lock and I can use it as a shield to protect me from an aggressor. The affordance is not simply a fixed or physical property of the object or the environment because it is related to the human agency that perceives what it offers. Different human agents will perceive different agency in different objects although they may learn, either by trial and error or from each other, what a specific object might afford.

Gibson, however, in describing the material world in terms of what it affords most adult human beings insists on treating it as constant and unchanging; 'An elongated object of moderate size and weight affords wielding. If used to hit or strike, it is a *club* or *hammer*' (1979: 133). But the catch in this account is the 'if used' which makes affordance difficult to operationalize in any definitional way. In general what an object affords is how it can be used by a human but this leaves open the issue of variability that Gibson does not confront; what I can wield as a hammer may not afford such use by my rather frail mother. The adjustable wrench in a toolbox may be finely engineered to be used for fitting on the hexagonal heads of nuts or bolts in order to turn them ... but it may also afford hitting nails in. The wrench is also a hammer if I so use it, even though the owner of the toolbox may be appalled at this 'misuse' of their wrench.

For Ian Hutchby (2001) it is the very resistance to cultural variability that is appealing about the concept of affordance in understanding technology as against those theories that rely on a textual metaphor to describe the social construction of technology (he uses Grint and Woolgar 1997 as an exemplar of this tendency). Affordance suggests a real, physical world in which objects are not reducible to texts that are always open to reinterpretation: 'different technologies possess different affordances, and these affordances *constrain the ways that they can possibly be "written" or "read"'* (Hutchby 2001: 447). The physical form of material objects constrains what they can be used for – a wrench may be used as a hammer but it cannot be used for sewing or boiling water in. Recent commentators like Hutchby and Costall (1995, 1997) are attracted by the concept of affordance and have attempted to 'socialise' it so that it can take account of cultural variability. Hutchby does this first by attempting to distinguish between 'social and technological rules' that delimit how an object is used and, second, by recognizing that affordance can be 'designed into' an artefact (Hutchby 2001: 449). The technological rules refer to what a human being can possibly do with an object – use a wrench as a hammer but not as a needle – and the social rules refer to moral constraints – I should not use someone else's wrench as a hammer. Alan Costall (1995, 1997) has also attempted to 'socialize' the concept of affordance by extending it to include 'learning' affordance from others, designing it in and specifying it by assigning meanings and functions to objects in the social world. In this social version of affordance there is a 'morality of things' (Costall 1995: 473) in which people police each other's uses of things – as when the owner of a wrench says something like, 'you're not going to use it to hammer that nail are you?' when I ask if I can borrow it. In shifting the concept of affordance from the physical to the social realm there is the risk of opening it up to infinite interpretability – exactly what Hutchby fears from the social constructionists. Costall's solution is to suggest that there is a cultural strategy that specifies the prime purposes of objects in terms of their 'canonical affordance' in which the name attached to an object defines the 'meaning' of an object and so what is should be used for (Costall 1997: 79). The wrench carries its name because it's canonical affordance is to *wrench* things, such as pipes, nuts or bolts which it grips and affords a lever for humans to turn or twist them with. Hammering is done with something called a hammer which would be its canonical affordance. The assigning of names to objects that are linked through the use of language to particular practical uses is one way of asserting the consistency of their physical and social functions. But this is some way from Gibson's idea of affordance which was precisely designed to specify human/object relations at the material level in terms of the perception of physical properties. Costall's reformulation helpfully draws out the social relations with objects – designing, making, adapting, learning to use, maintaining, policing and so on – but then leaves 'affordance' as a fluid concept that is subject to interpretation and textualization which is precisely what Hutchby wanted to protect Gibson's concept from.

While Hutchby wants to use affordance to settle the physical properties of an object in relation to human beings, it is impossible to get around the reinterpretation of physical objects that occurs in their context of design and use and which specifies their function and so what they actually afford.[7] Costall's introduction of the 'morality of things' moves the discussion of the agency of objects a long way from the idea of affordance. For Gibson it was simply a matter of perception – which he treated as a material function of the human animal in which objects give out 'stimulus information' (1979: 140). What he did not seem to recognize, despite his 'ecological' perspective, is that culture informs our perception, affecting the way we see the world. As our organs of perception develop physically within the body we *learn* how to use them from the cultural context of the society around us. Other species also learn from their parents and other members of their social group to use their bodies in certain ways. Some other species have developed the capacity to use material objects in their environment to extend their agency; thrushes and sea otters using a stone to break shells, chimps using leaves as shelters and grass stems as termite gathering divides.[8] But it is human beings that have become supreme at creating material objects to meet their purposes; here, imagination and mind create affordance at the immaterial level and continually mould and remould the material world to achieve that effect. Neither the material world nor the way that humans perceive it is sufficiently stable in the face of cultural modification to be determinative of what things can do.

The actor-network

The concept of affordance is tempting because it seems to offer a way of talking about the agency of objects and how they interact with humans at the material level. At the end of the twentieth century it seemed to attract a revival of interest outside the psychology of perception from commentators, including Hutchby and Costall, as a way of resisting the direction taken by the sociology of technology over recent decades. Trevor Pinch and Wiebe Bijker (1987) explain how the sociology of technology had developed from empirical and theoretical work in the sociology of science and in the history of technology. Sociologists of science had traditionally restricted themselves to studying the social context of science; institutional, political and funding arrangements. However, by the 1980s they were arguing that scientific discovery was not an internal matter of scientific practice leading systematically to the truth but was a process of 'social construction' through which 'truth' was distinguished from 'falsity'. The effect of a number of substantive studies by historians and sociologists was profound, as Pinch and Bijker put it: 'scientific knowledge can be, and indeed has been shown to be thoroughly socially constituted ... there is nothing epistemologically special about the nature of scientific knowledge' (1987: 19). This opening up of the practices of science as ways of understanding the material world was linked to changes in the approach to the history of technology that also began to explore the social contingencies that surround the emergence of new technologies (e.g. Hughes 1983, 1987). In place of the backwards reconstruction of technological successes that had been the standard approach, a new history of technology was interested in how social relations shaped new technologies. This shift in the approach to science and technology changed how social and technological relations were understood and began to turn attention towards the objects in themselves.

   The undermining of science as having the exclusive epistemological warrant to study how humans dealt with the material world opened the way for research that addressed the impact of social factors on emerging technologies, both those that succeeded and those that failed. Pinch and Bijker argued that it was not simply discoveries about the nature of things

that leads to technological development because social, political and economic influences affect where and how human energies, ingenuity and
effort are invested and which discoveries are then seized upon and
approved. They called their programme for investigating technology in
society the Social Construction of Technology (SCOT) programme and suggested 'not only that there is flexibility in how people think of or interpret
artefacts but also that there is flexibility in how artefacts are *designed*' (1987:
40). They used the development of the bicycle to show how different types
of bicycle were developed, all of which worked but each of which was
subject to different cultural interpretations. It was the competition between
these interpretations rather than a rational technical progression that led to
the eclipse of the upright, exciting and dangerous 'penny farthing' bicycle
by the modern 'safety' bicycle with two wheels of the same size and pedals
driving through a chain and gear mechanism. The different interpretations
were not generated simply in the minds of engineers or technologists but
came from users and commentators, such as those writing in newspapers
and magazines. The issues of safety and comfort interacted with those of
speed and excitement, gender and age to create a range of responses to different bicycle designs. The language that Pinch and Bijker used to describe
the technological development of the bicycle (interpretive flexibility,
rhetorical closure, redefinition of the problem) was more reminiscent of the
analysis of a narrative than of practical, technological decisions.

    If Pinch and Bijker summarized a shift towards recognizing the impor-
tance of interpretation in socially constructing the path of technological
development, Thomas Hughes (1983, 1987) pointed to the interconnectedness of causal processes impacting together as systems. Both these shifts
disturbed the rational, sequential, progressive model of technology as a
linear sequence of actions that solved problems to arrive at a final solution.
Hughes, writing about electricity and the light bulb from a historical perspective, pointed out the systemic and interdependent relationship
between the light bulb and the distribution of electricity; for one to be
developed it needed the other. Both are aspects of the same system and all
the technological problems across the system need to be solved before any
part of the system can be said to function. Instead of the metaphors of narrative analysis, Hughes introduced the military phrase 'reverse salient' to
refer to the interruptions in smooth technological progress that often have
ramifications that are not simply solved by redesign since other parts of the
system are always implicated. What works for one part of the system does
not necessarily work for another part and 'reverse salients are components
in the system that have fallen behind or are out of phase with the others'
(1987: 73). Hughes's systems include both artefacts and humans so that in
an electricity distribution system, for example, the 'load-dispatching center
with its communication and control artifacts' switches a system of other
objects such as turbines, and generators but is also 'part of a hierarchical

control system involving the management structure of the utility' (1987: 54). The utility itself will involve industrial scientists, engineers, managers, and workers who are integrated into a larger social system of entrepreneurs, businesses, advertisers, investors, government departments and consumers that is in turn integrated into the material system of the various interconnected pieces of equipment. Any one of these human or technical subsystems may generate a reverse salient and trying to remove it is almost certain to affect every other part of the system.

The impact of the social construction of technology thesis, allied with Hughes's approach to technology as both physical and social system, was to alter the relationship between sociology and technology that I discussed in Chapter 3. The empirical studies in the history and sociology of science began to offer support for the idea that technology is always cultural and social and thus irreducible to its internal material features, which had been a feature of the critiques of technology by Mumford, Heidegger, Marcuse and Ellul. Instead of technology being something counterposed to society that might determine it or be more or less 'autonomous', the social studies of technology that emerged in the late 1980s began to show how society and technology are integrated and mutually determining. A number of edited collections brought together historians and social scientists interested in rethinking technology to address its political, moral and social effects and influences in a radically new way (MacKenzie and Wajcman 1985; Callon et al. 1986; Bijker et al. 1987; Law 1991; Bijker and Law 1992). This rethinking of society and technology emphasized how, far from being determined by technology, society was a major force in shaping technology. This displaced both the model of technology as the invention of individual minds blessed with creativity and imagination and the model of technological knowledge as an adjunct to scientific knowledge about the material world in which everything was there, waiting to be discovered like a lost continent or the structure of DNA.

From within the new social studies of science a distinctive version emerged that was particularly associated with the French authors Bruno Latour, Michelle Callon and Madeleine Akrich and came to be known as 'Actor-Network Theory' or ANT. These authors took the themes of Hughes's systems and Pinch and Bijker's SCOT approach but shifted the emphasis towards the material artefacts to suggest that their agency was often as potent in a network of actors as that of the human participants. The 'actants' or 'non-humans' that feature in ANT studies include living organisms (microbes – Latour 1988a; scallops – Callon 1986b) as well as physical objects (electric cars – Callon 1986a; transit systems – Latour 1996; lighting systems – Akrich 1992; aircraft – Law and Callon 1992). The non-humans are intermingled with humans to form a network so, for example, in Callon's study of the attempt to develop an electric car in 1970s' France, there are 'accumulators, fuel cells, electrodes, electrons, catalysts and electrolytes' in addition to consumers, companies and ministries (1986a: 22). Sometimes the non-humans appear to display intention – Michel Callon writes that the scallops in St. Brieuc bay 'must first be willing to anchor themselves' (1986b: 211) – but this can only amount to saying that within the network the non-humans act *as if* they had intention. What is innovative in ANT is recognizing that both humans and non-humans in the network can resist or enhance technological development and the interplay between one and the other produces the effects of what Hughes calls 'reverse salients'. Social forces such as the presence – or lack – of cash or political enthusiasm, interplay with technical forces such as the way that fuel cells or electrolytes work as hoped – or not – to create the technology … or not. The network may be understood as ultimately infinite since technologies interplay with the material world and social actors participate in various complex relations that may be cultural or political at, finally, a global level (Law and Callon 1992). However, ANT has a way of dealing with the potentially infinite proliferation of actors and networks; it 'black-boxes' sub-networks that appear, or are presented, as a single entity within a particular network (Callon et al. 1986: xvi; Latour 1999: 304).

There are two departures in ANT from both the traditional social and historical study of technology and the 'systems' and SCOT approaches of Hughes, Pinch and Bijker discussed above. In ANT, the non-humans are treated as if they had autonomous agency; they appear to act as if they exercised will or intention. For example, in an illustration that Latour draws on a number of times, a mechanical door-closer, sometimes referred to as a 'groom', is shown to be treated as if it were a human actor by human actors in the setting (1988b, 1992a). Latour tells us about a 'small written notice: "The Groom is On Strike, For God's Sake, Keep The Door Closed"' that was posted on the door of a room in which a meeting was taking place (1992a: 227). The door provided a way of allowing humans to pass through walls and yet close the gap behind them and the 'groom' or door closer substituted for humans having to remember and expend effort to close the door. With the door closed, noise and drafts could be kept out and those inside can work in peace; the 'groom' accepted the 'delegation' of the task of shutting the door ('every time you want to know what a non-human does, simply imagine what other humans or non-humans would have to do were this character not present', Latour 1992: 229). The door could be closed by whoever goes through it or a particular human could be assigned to the task of being doorman to open and close it for others and Latour is able to point out that non-humans in this way enter into human relations of power. To assign someone the task of being doorman is to exert power over them and to assign the task to a mechanical door closer is for it to exert power over those using the door. This is a physical power that may not be easy for the weak – children, frail people or those in wheelchairs – to overcome but it ensures that after all who enter, the door is kept closed. Latour and Akrich call this process by which the artefact works back on humans 'prescription' because it involves moral as well as physical effects; doors with 'grooms' *shall* be kept closed (1992).

The example nicely illustrates how humans and non-humans are intertwined in a set of relations that amount to a network in which it is difficult to identify precisely where the agency for actions lies. Latour introduces the idea of non-humans substituting for humans which is a characteristic feature of much technology, especially that which seems to operate autonomously or independently of a human operator. He also raises the issues of power and morality, showing that material objects become vehicles of social rules that are applied to humans and intervene in power relationships between people. People have to learn to act in accordance with rules and in accordance with the way that non-humans operate – people have to learn to get through the door smartly or the door closer will catch them. It is, Latour argues, an increase in the population of non-humans that increases the 'sum of morality' (1992: 232) and comprises the 'hidden and despised social masses' (1992: 227) that sociologists have failed to identify in the modern world. The metaphor that Latour and his ANT colleagues frequently use to describe how non-humans are caught up in society is that of 'inscription'; the actions that have moral effects in our culture are inscribed within the material objects that are produced in our culture. Latour is keen on how objects police behaviour: road signs, blocks to prevent parking on sidewalks, seatbelts and, one of his favourite examples, the 'sleeping policeman' (1992: 244; 1999: 188). The traffic authorities build the speed bump to slow down cars and thereby inscribe within it the moral injunction that might be expressed by a real policeman or in a road sign. The material object of the speed bump, road sign or speed camera 'stands in for an actor and creates an asymmetry between absent makers and occasional users' (1999: 189). Moral authority is delegated to the materiality of the speed bump which enforces it physically by jarring the bodies of drivers and damaging their cars if they don't slow down. The delegated moral authority of speed cameras is sometimes transposed into legal action while interactive speed signs simply remind the driver of their moral duty.

Despite Hutchby's complaints about the use of the textual metaphor in ANT, it does allow for the variability of interpretation of material objects which often depends on where the interpreter is in the network. Objects are reinterpreted and rendered as 'texts' in a variety of ways including reports, diagrams, plans and of course their material instantiation – Latour's (1996) rather long-winded account of the failed Aramis urban transport system demonstrates the variety of textual forms and interpretations that emerged in the network. ANT incorporates both Hughes's important recognition that the material technologies of late modernity are increasingly interconnected as systems and it allows for a 'social construction' of technology that breaks from the traditional linear account of rational progress. And it goes further by disturbing the separation that Hughes maintains between those systems that are material and those that are social by suggesting that determination of technological change does not lie in its social dimensions but may come from either both material or social entities. The effect of these two modifications to the new programme in the social approach to technology set out by Pinch and Bijker (1987) is to attribute a level of agency to the material objects in technological networks that had been more or less absent before. This agency can be expressed as a moral quality that feeds back on human actors through 'prescriptions' so that it is never clear precisely where the moral force originates; is it in human decisions or is it in the serendipitous quality of artefacts? But what ANT fails to do is to study closely the interaction or the lived relationship between human beings and material objects. The empirical work is by and large lacking the detail and precision of the more traditional social studies of technology and many of the textual productions and interpretations are those of the sociologist rather than the actors. It is noticeable that there are very few accounts of the perceptual or tactile interaction between humans and objects in the network, few detailed field observations, photographs or use of video to study the process of the network that would allow the material objects to have a presence in the accounts.[9] What are found in the published studies, are textual forms that are produced sometimes by the human participants – engineers' reports, publicity statements, transcripts of discussions, summatory diagrams – but often by the sociologist. These can be excitingly irreverent, entertainingly laden with irony and wit and full of interesting conceptual moves – but these textual devices keep the sociologist in control of the play of interpretations and keep the reader at a safe distance from the lived workings of the network.

Conclusion

Elsewhere (Dant 2004) I have discussed Gibson's affordances and actor network theory in the context of considering how useful they are in understanding the assemblage of a human driver and a motor car that I have called the 'driver-car'. As against Gibson's account of driving in which it is the driver's perception that is paramount, ANT does encourage us to recognize that the car and its material form interact with the driver to produce a network in which moral authority is exchanged between the two. Latour (1992a) discusses how the integration of seatbelts with the car ignition or a sound alarm is fine tuned to make the exertion of moral authority over the driver acceptable; if it is too irritating it will be turned off or removed. In another classic problem of the dispersal of moral responsibility between the agency of humans and non-humans, Latour asks whether it is guns or people who kill: 'Which of them, then, the gun or the citizen, is the *actor* in this situation? *Someone else* (a citizen-gun, a gun-citizen)' (1999: 179). As Latour points out, the human agent is transformed by the possession of the gun, but the gun is also transformed by being in the hand of someone willing to use it. The possible actions of both human and non-human are transformed by their combination into an assemblage but the difference between humans and non-humans is left unclear. For example, with the citizen-gun, Latour asserts: 'Purposeful action and intentionality may not be properties of objects, but they are not properties of humans either' and suggests that it is only corporate bodies that can bear the burden of intentionality; individual decisions are always made in a legitimating social context (1999: 192–3).[10]

To say that a gun affords killing is to say very little since it also affords not killing but this does not stop Hutchby from claiming that the material level of affordance is paramount: 'the fact that a bullet fired from a gun has effects on flesh and bone that are intrinsic to the gun and the bullet ... cannot be altered by social construction' (2001: 446). Indeed, once the bullet has left the gun, we could say that it affords terrible injury or death to any animal in its path but while the bullet remains within the gun its affordance is in abeyance; it may prove a very effective and safe deterrent against an armed criminal. Alfred Gell has also commented on the same issue of responsibility in discussing weapons and those who use them. He ties the 'secondary agency' in the gun and the bullet to the 'primary agency' of whoever uses it so that it is clear that the soldier has the responsibility for a resulting death. But, as he puts it 'The soldier's weapons are *parts* of him which make him what he is' (Gell 1998: 20–1). The soldier may carry the moral responsibility but the thing enables the formation of an assemblage that has certain capabilities and this fits with Warnier's praxeological account of the carrier of a gun as becoming 'fused with his material culture' in everyday life (2001: 21 – see Chapter 1).

In an important sense all these perspectives are pertinent to understanding how materiality becomes entwined with sociality and no one perspective is paramount. Although his analysis is mostly concerned with the emotional life of the individual, Tisseron reminds us that the interactions between individuals and objects are not simply practical but are the way that the emotional core of our beings is connected to the culture beyond us. Alfred Gell shows how objects acquire agency that is not reducible to their symbolic form and alerts us to how person-hood can be distributed through material objects. The concept of affordance is ultimately unsatisfying because it equivocates about the flexibility of materiality in the light of culture but it does make us look closely at the materiality of objects and how they are fitted into human action. ANT reminds us of the complexity of relations between humans and artefacts so that we can neither be sure where responsibility or cause originates nor that sociality emerges through the interaction between the two. But ANT is rather too concerned with the transient nature of textual forms and pays little attention to the material level of how human beings engage with things. Instead of seeing materiality as being juxtaposed to society, it needs to be seen as an expression of both individuality and society. It is ultimately a question of existence; the material world is not distinct from the social world and nor can material entities be treated as in any simple way distinct from human ones. In the next chapter I will consider how the being-in-the-world that is human and social is always and already cast in relation to the materiality of that world.

5   Being-with materiality

Introduction

Writing about technology and society has, as we saw in Chapter 3, largely taken the problems and issues to be of a wholly social nature, usually treating the material world of technology as somehow in opposition to the social world of people. The main focus of those debates is on the political realm and concerns the gross impacts of technology on society in the flow of history. However, the debate about whether the social world shapes technology or whether technology shapes the social world actually pays very little attention to the interface between people and their material world. Recent debates about the material world have begun to focus more closely on this interface by looking at the distribution of agency between people and things which I discussed in Chapter 4. In the present chapter I want to take that focus closer still by thinking about the interrelationship between society as the lived-in bodies of people and the material world as the entities that they encounter. It is this interaction between people as material bodies and things as material bodies that is the stuff of technology and the material culture of a society. Because it is so close to the ordinary flow of life, it is easy to take for granted and treat as something about which we already know because it is so familiar. And yet it is in this taking for granted of our material, embodied relationships with things that we can so easily overlook the way that our material culture gives substance to the society we live in.

To begin to look closer at this embodied, material relationship between people and things I want to go back, both historically and to the simplest and most basic aspects of the materiality of social action, to recover the phenomenology of Martin Heidegger, whose later critique of technology was discussed in Chapter 3, and the distinctive account of perception and embodiment to be found in the writing of Maurice Merleau-Ponty. This philosophically informed perspective will lay the groundwork for the study of material interaction in Chapter 6.

Being with objects

It is not the intention here to provide a detailed account of Heidegger's early philosophy either in general or as it relates to the material world (see Ihde 1990; Dreyfus 1991). Instead I will do considerable violence to the coherence of Heidegger's monumental *Being and Time* (1962) by dragging some of his concepts and remarks from the text to help in understanding how human beings relate to objects.

Dealing with things

To proceed with his inquiry into the everydayness of Being-in-the-world, Heidegger asks what the entities within the world are and what their characteristics as Being are, and how they constitute the 'environment' of Dasein (1962: 93–95).[1] His answer is that it is through our 'dealings' with the things in the world in which we are immersed in everyday life that they have ontological significance for us. Environment for Heidegger is not just there, it does not have its own intrinsic qualities, but is oriented to the concerns of the being who is dealing with it: 'The kind of dealing which is closest to us is as we have shown, not a bare perceptual cognition, but rather that kind of concern which manipulates things and puts them to use; and this has its own kind of "knowledge"' (Heidegger 1962: 95).

'Concern' (*Besorgen*) is, as always with Heidegger, a very specific word which does not translate directly; it is one of the ways of being-in-the-world for Dasein, with a more practical and less emotional connotation than the English word, and refers to actions including producing something, looking after something or making use of something.[2] Whereas we might begin by listing or naming the things we could see in our environment, Heidegger begins by pointing to our lived relationship with them. He avoids a simple theoretical account and suggests that how the material world exists for us is constituted in our practical actions and how we make use of the things around us. Rather than seeing things as having intrinsic value, he sees them as significant for Dasein through how they are incorporated into everyday activities as *Zeug* – usually translated as 'equipment' but more analogous to 'stuff', 'gear' or 'implements', that is, things that are used for a purpose and are handled.

In thinking about the material world of a garage technician, for example, we can imagine that his environment is taken for granted in that it is familiar and unremarkable.[3] For an outsider the large space is quite remarkable with its high ambient noise levels (radio, amplified telephone bells, engine noises, power tools, etc.); its mixture of natural light, fluorescent light and dark spaces; its variety of hard surfaces of brick and metal; and its fullness with objects that are specific to the environment (tools and toolboxes of various sizes and equipment such as hydraulic lifts). But for those who spend their working week in such a space, its structural order is created by what they do in the space and how they take up things to work with, how they move through the space and how things are placed relative to each other. As Heidegger puts it, the characteristics of 'thinghood' and 'reality' are 'substantiality, materiality, extendedness, side-by-sideness, and so forth' (1962: 96). The things in the environment are constituted through how they fit into the process of what the technician does: 'Equipment is essentially "something in order to...". A totality is constituted by various ways of the "in-order-to", such as serviceability, conduciveness, usability, manipulability' (Heidegger 1962: 97). For Heidegger, 'equipmentality' is never singular; one piece of equipment is always related to other equipment and this is always the case in garages where one tool is selected from an extensive range of possible tools.

It is precisely in terms of a hand tool, a hammer, that Heidegger famously explains how equipment is incorporated into actions:

> Equipment can genuinely show itself only in dealings cut to its own measure (hammering with a hammer, for example); but in such dealings an entity of this kind is not *grasped* thematically as an occurring Thing, nor is the equipment-structure known as such even in the using. The hammering does not simply have knowledge about the hammer's character as equipment, but it has appropriated this equipment in a way which could not possibly be more suitable.
>
> (Heidegger 1962: 98)

This passage extends the distinction that Heidegger makes between the material object as a Thing and its significance as equipment to human beings. But there are three other aspects that he is pointing out here that I would like to emphasize. First, he is pointing out that the material world is of interest to Dasein in terms of *acting* in the world. This is an embodied and material action which happens in time; the state of concrete, material things are altered through Dasein's action and equipment is incorporated into that action. Second, he is pointing to the knowledge that is part of this process of action; Dasein knows what a hammer can do and that is part of its equipmentality. However, that knowledge is embodied rather than brought to consciousness as a thought or an idea – it is disclosed to Dasein as for use in this type of action. Third, there is a meeting of Dasein and the equipmentality of the hammer in the action that appropriates it and uses it as something which 'could not possibly be more suitable'. Even if it is a successful appropriation, it is not predetermined; the head of the hammer might have fallen off at the first blow, the hammer might be too small for what it is to hit. The type of knowledge involved here is not *of* the object but *in* the action; 'hammering' is not an intrinsic property either of Dasein or of the object but are aspects of the human/object relation that are essential to being-in-the-world and are only fully realized in an active relationship between the material object and the embodied being that is Dasein.

Readiness-to-hand

Equipment has its own form of being that is not determined by its designed-in or its physical properties. For Heidegger, the things in the world are available to Dasein as equipment through their 'readiness-to-hand' which both draws attention to their physical proximity to the human body and to their significance as usable with that body for action.[4] With Heidegger's hammer it is the 'hammering itself that uncovers the specific "manipulability" of the hammer' and so reveals the being of the hammer as equipment that he calls 'readiness-to-hand' (1962: 98). Just looking at something, even looking at things 'theoretically', is not the same as 'dealing' with them. In a common-sense mode, when we turn our attention to the world and the things in it, we apprehend it as a series of things in themselves with properties of colour, shape, size, and so on. This is what Heidegger refers to as 'presence-at-hand' but his phenomenology of Being points out that this is a second-order appropriation of the world that stands back to think about it rather than living in it.[5] That thinking, he says, is founded on a prior appropriation of the world as 'ready-to-hand' in which things are taken up in use and activity: 'To lay bare what is just "present-at-hand" and no more, cognition must first penetrate *beyond* what is ready-to-hand in our concern' (Heidegger 1962: 101).

The sociologist in a garage takes up a reflexive mode, trying to grasp it as present-at-hand, looking at a spanner and imagining how it might be applied to a particular nut.[6] But the mechanic simply takes up the spanner or puts together the socket set without imagining or theorizing how it is to be used, demonstrating that this is equipment that is ready-to-hand: 'The ready-to-hand is not grasped theoretically at all ... The peculiarity of what is proximally ready-to-hand is that, in its readiness to hand, it must, as it were, withdraw in order to be ready to hand quite authentically' (Heidegger 1962: 99). In choosing a tool technicians did not measure the nut to be worked on and rarely looked at the size markings on a socket or a spanner. Their embodied knowledge of the task in hand enabled them to choose the appropriate type of socket, extension, lever or power driver and the one they needed usually 'withdrew' from those around it. Heidegger's phrase, 'ready-to-hand' reminds us that the orientation of material things in the world to Dasein is embodied and engaged; it is through touch, through manipulability, through bringing them into the body, as into the hand, or at least into contact with the body, that they break free from the environment and have relevance as a distinct entity. To be available as ready-to-hand, things are identified through what Heidegger calls 'circumspection' – a form of sight that includes both 'looking around' and 'in order to'. Here Heidegger's jargon reminds us of the unremarkable way in which sight and touch are part of each other and both are part of action that realizes Being in the world. Rather than a distinctive action of looking, a looking that is an action complete in itself, 'circumspection' is that form of sight which is part of the flow of a familiar action. Circumspection is a bodily capacity to orient the material form of the body – including its brain – to other material entities that may be partly achieved through a movement of the whole body and even of the hands rather than through some specific action of the eyes or the organs of sight. On a number of occasions in our corpus of data we see technicians looking through boxes of tools or collections of parts that have been removed and set out on the floor. The mechanic moves his body, his head and the tools or parts as he looks through them in a very clear form of 'circumspection' in that he is trying to draw into his hand – quite literally – the appropriate object for his next task.[7]

It is concern with things that organizes circumspection but sometimes what is needed for the task in hand is not available; it may be broken or simply missing. Such things identify themselves with a quality of 'unreadiness-to-hand' as they become conspicuous and stand in the way of the work proceeding.[8] Now for Heidegger this makes both the thing and the task for which it was needed become explicit, so he says that the context of equipment is 'lit up' and 'the world announces itself' when something is unready-to-hand (1962: 105). As the flow of work is interrupted, the task becomes something different and the way that the world of things and activities is appropriated by the person becomes 'thematic', that is, it is the thing in-itself that becomes of concern as its brokenness or absence has to be dealt with. It is at the point when something goes wrong that the human has to stand back in a reflective mode and consider what things are, that the world becomes present-at-hand and objects take on qualities as things in themselves. So what happens when the missing tool or a replacement part is found? Heidegger explains that Dasein inhabits the world spatially, and things are brought into readiness-at-hand by their movement in space that he calls 'de-severance' [Ent-fernung] or 'abolishing their remoteness'.[9] This is not to do with objective, physical space but to do with drawing the thing into the current action: 'for the most part, de-severing is a circumspective bringing-close – bringing something close by, in the sense of procuring it, putting it in readiness, having it to hand' (Heidegger 1962: 139–40). Then the work can proceed.

Merleau-Ponty

Although Heidegger's investigation of Being is concerned with far more than the few concepts I have extracted from it, it is significant that he begins his phenomenology by trying to grasp the relationship of human being to the material environment and the things within it. It is clear that he sees this relationship as embodied from the start; it is precisely not with conceptual thought or knowledge that our engagement with the world around us begins. However, Heidegger has very little to say about the physicality of embodied being and how this shapes our relations with the material world. Maurice Merleau-Ponty responds precisely to this theme in his major work, *Phenomenology of Perception* (1962), which attempts to address the link between the 'in-itself' of being-in-the-world and the being-for-itself of conscious reflection, by analysing phenomenologically the relationship between the inside and the outside of the body.[10]

Just as Heidegger's ontology begins by stressing the continuity between what we can recognize as human being and its material environment through its ordinary action, Merleau-Ponty stresses the integration between the exterior world that is made available to perception and the interiority of human being. In doing so he is going against two strands of scientific thought which had presented very different perspectives on human engagement with the world. On the one hand was the 'behaviourist' who saw the body as a mechanistic system that responded to stimuli with autonomic responses – a system that could be explained in terms of functionalist rationality. On the other was the 'mentalist' who saw the body as a system driven by a brain processing information received through the senses before deciding how to act. Both perspectives set apart human being and the world it inhabits as entities in themselves – 'There was no longer any real *for-itself* other than the thought of the scientist which perceives the system and which alone ceases to occupy any place in it. Thus, while the living body became an exterior without interior, subjectivity became interior without exterior, an impartial spectator' (1962: 56). Merleau-Ponty was in good company in this critique of both behaviourism and psychologism; the American traditions of symbolic interactionism and pragmatism (particularly the writing of Mead 1962, 1980) and the European ordinary language tradition of philosophy are also deeply critical of both these 'scientistic' approaches to understanding human being. But what is distinctive about Merleau-Ponty's response to the two scientistic traditions is his focus on the materiality of the body; questions of consciousness, of self, of mind and of being cannot be addressed independently of the embodied form they take.

Form

Merleau-Ponty emphasizes the body as an integrated whole so that 'subsystems' such as perceptual senses, the motor system or cognition cannot be considered as independent and linked by mechanical connections. This holistic approach owes much to Gestalt psychology, so he argues that what affects one part of the body's being interacts with all other parts which together constitute a form: 'there is a form whenever the properties of a system are modified by every change brought about in a single one of its parts and, on the contrary, are conserved when they all change while maintaining the same relationship among themselves' (Merleau-Ponty 1983: 47). The idea of the form is that the whole is greater than the sum of its parts and is counterposed to a functionalist or anatomical perspective that breaks down the whole into sub-systems but Merleau-Ponty is going further in suggesting that the structure of *behaviour* takes on the quality of a form; it is not mind that directs body or body which acts mindlessly. Much of what Merleau-Ponty has to say about the structure of behaviour could be applied equally to other animals as to human beings – all animals, and no doubt many other higher organisms, respond to the world as a form that produces patterned behaviour. My cat will look at the chair and then at the radiator and appear to 'decide' (I have no idea what mental process are involved) where to sit. Whether the radiator is on, whether the chair is warm from having been sat in, will affect the resulting action but not in a simple determinative way that could be exactly predicted. Once the 'decision' is made, the cat's motor processes of getting to the spot and getting comfortable also follow a form or pattern but are never precisely repeats of what she did last time.

This sort of structured behaviour we share with cats but Merleau-Ponty distinguishes a type of behaviour that we do not share with animals but which is nonetheless structured in a remarkably similar way.[11] This is the symbolic interpretation of signs. Animals respond to signs (the fridge door works for my cat) but not symbols; for Merleau-Ponty one way that this distinction is realized is that a symbol for a human being becomes the 'proper theme of an activity which tends to *express* it' (1983: 120). He gives the example of reading music to play an instrument in which there is a direct correlation between a symbol (a musical note) and a motor action. The experienced musician simply plays the music without translating individual notes into particular actions but this is not simply a subconscious mechanical response because the player is aware of the form and will usually notice a transcription error as a deviation from it. Indeed, the same sorts of actions lie behind an interpretation of the written music and the player who knows how to play an instrument could even construct melodies by 'improvising' without the symbols being present at all. This capacity to improvise can also be independent of the instrument so that a musician (Merleau-Ponty uses the example of an organist) can play on an instrument they have never encountered before. Provided that it has the form of an instrument they are familiar with, the improviser can produce music that has never been played before: 'The character of the melody, the graphic configuration of the musical text and the unfolding of the gestures participate in a single structure, have in common a single nucleus of signification' (Merleau-Ponty 1983: 121). What 'music' is cannot be reduced to any one of these three interconnected systems – melody, musical text, bodily gesture – and they share a single structure, a single 'nucleus of signification'.

In the garage we saw precisely this human capacity as the technicians worked on makes and models of cars that they had not seen before with considerable confidence. The braking systems, the steering mechanisms, exhaust pipe and the fuel systems, for example, are much the same on most cars and can be treated as part of a form. They may be of different sizes and types of materials and they may not be fitted in precisely the same way – the number and location of bolts may vary, for example. But nonetheless, cleaning brakes, replacing exhaust pipes, and so on are routine tasks which the technicians we observed were happy to carry out on just about any vehicle they were presented with. With an unusual vehicle, much like Merleau-Ponty's organist, they would inspect it briefly before deciding whether or not they could proceed as usual. In the main, technicians used the 'gestures' that they knew were effective in proceeding with a task, much as we can imagine that an organist would have a number of standard tunes 'at their fingertips' and not require any sheet music or improvisatory skills. But there were occasions when we saw technicians resorting to the sheet music of their skill; the manuals that gave measurement tolerances, torque settings and diagrams showing the arrangement and interconnection of components and fixings. There were also many occasions when things were not exactly as expected and they had to 'improvise', or feel their way through the task. On these sorts of occasions they would often ask colleagues for advice and in many instances in the data we can see brief consultations during which they are attempting to grasp the form – both material and symbolic – of the task in hand.

Embodiment

Our bodies are material entities but are, for us, not quite like any other thing. As Merleau-Ponty puts it, the body is 'that by which there are objects. It is neither tangible nor visible in so far as it is that which sees and touches' (1962: 92). The reason why I cannot observe my body in the same way as I can observe other things is because it is my body that I use to take up a perspective: to look from this angle, to redirect my gaze, to stand back, to move closer. And the same happens when I look in the mirror; seen in the mirror, my body 'never stops following my intentions like their shadow' (Merleau-Ponty 1962: 91). Of course the parts of the body can be viewed as objects – so I can look at my hands and turn them over much as I might any other manipulable object – but the body as a whole cannot be seen in this way. The body in the mirror is no more than a simulacrum that 'refers me back to an original of the body which is not there among things, but in my own province, on this side of all things seen' (Merleau-Ponty 1962: 92).

It is our body that situates all other objects in space and time and provides us with a perspective through which we can judge the relative position of other objects. Touch as well as sight are the means through which I make contact with the outside world and even contact with myself; my right hand can touch my left. For Merleau-Ponty the capacity to touch is an orientation rather than simply a response of nerves in the skin so I can put my hands together and they can alternate the roles of touching and being touched. In the same way, pain in an extremity is not felt as the source of pain to some inner being, the pain is felt in the locality in which it is. And again, the awareness of movement in my body is not of something being moved, as might be the case if I were to move an object, but is awareness of me moving – as he says 'I have no need to look for it, it is already with me – I do not need to lead it towards the movement's completion, it is in contact with it from the start and propels itself towards that end' (Merleau-Ponty 1962: 94).

The sense of being a body that is not divided into parts or organs, that is complete with all its parts interior to itself and therefore always distinguishable from objects which are outside, is what is involved in having a 'corporeal schema' or 'body image'. The body image is that part of being that means we always know where we are; we can feel the space that we inhabit in the world. For Merleau-Ponty, body image or body cenethesis[12] is not a construct that is the product of sensory information, of growing awareness, or cumulative experience but is in some way anterior to the sensori-motor unity of the body. It is only through the completeness of the body image, the sense of being in *this* body, that I can have awareness of what is exterior to it. Body image is then to do with the spatiality of situation rather than position ('where am I?', not 'where is it?') and yet it can be dynamic as when my body takes up a situation in relation to other objects and my body image is oriented to them according to its actions. In this sense Merleau-Ponty describes the body as being a 'third term' in the figure-background structure; the body faces 'figures' which stand in front of it and 'backgrounds' is what is beyond them. It is from the situation of the body in space that all other orientations follow and make sense: top and bottom, right and left, in front and behind.

The concept of embodiment that Merleau-Ponty establishes is that of a phenomenal body that can be contrasted with a scientifically apprehended body. The latter will have a determinate structure, a geometrical form, specifiable qualities and limitations and could be summarized by a series of measurements. But the phenomenal body is present to us as beings-in-the-world as something not only involved in a concrete setting, in relation to a situation and to tasks but also 'open to those verbal and imaginary situations which he can choose for himself or which may be suggested to him' (Merleau-Ponty 1962: 108). The phenomenal body can then reckon with the possible and entertain possible actions as extending from the current situation and tasks.

Field

For us our bodies are permanent, always present and the means through which a phenomenal field is apparent to us – and in that sense our body cannot be a part of that phenomenal field. Merleau-Ponty argues that the only way to approach the relationship between human being and other beings in the world is through understanding the 'phenomenal field' that emerges through lived experience to produce the system 'self–others–things'. As against classical, objective science this involves

> [a] return to the world of actual experience which is prior to the objective world, since it is in it that we shall be able to grasp the theoretical basis no less than the limits of that objective world, restore things to their concrete physiognomy, to organisms their individual ways of dealing with the world, and to subjectivity its inherence in history.
>
> (Merleau-Ponty 1962: 57)

The language of a science, such as the measurements of ergonomics, will produce a very limited account, fixed like a snapshot, whereas Merleau-Ponty's concept of the 'phenomenal field' relocates us in the position of the perceiving, experiencing being that apprehends the material and social world as it acts within it. Lived experience involves the process of time so that 'field' always has the character of an incomplete space that evolves. Things are not discrete entities, although they may well be distinct beings, because they always exist in relationship with each other and in relation to the perceiving being. This 'gestalt' of relationships is what the 'phenomenal field' is; a patterning of the experienced world that is partly material but not exclusively so. Things and other beings are related to each other and to the perceiving being, through their associations and connections both in the present and in the past. The 'phenomenal field' of garage technician might include other technicians, customers and administrative staff, but it always includes the material objects (cars, tools, equipment) and the material environment (sounds, smells, textures, spaces). It will also contain traces of his past experiences of that space: paths taken, work done, talk uttered and tools used that give it meaning and a temporal depth.

Much of the interaction within the field will be between human beings and material objects but there are also social interactions between technicians, customers, foremen, managers, and so on. For a given technician their phenomenal field, for long periods of time, will be the underneath or the inside spaces of a car and various zones nearby (workbench, toolbox, array of parts) – the field is not, however, an 'inner world' or a mental fact but a lived-in space. The objective sciences of physics and engineering have much to say about the causes of wear or damage to a car that could be linked to the appropriate repair. But such accounts are of limited use in understanding what the car technician actually does, or how they grasp the situation in their phenomenal field and develop a course of action. How they perceive a task is determined not by scientific principles but by how they usually carry out their work in that particular field. And while their normal courses of action may have been influenced by scientific principles, it is their routine way of responding to objects and events within the field that will shape how their work proceeds.

Perception

The 'mentalist' psychologist tries to identify cognitive processes that respond to information received from the senses to direct attention, attribute meaning and make judgements. But Merleau-Ponty argues that these cannot be distinguished as mental events that happen independently from perception because they are entailed in the very process of perceiving. Every perception involves attention being directed towards something, 'sense' being made of it and a judgement arrived at, at least to distinguish one thing from another.[13] Perception is not, for example, separate from the body's motor system; what the eyes see is not simply what is put in front of them but is connected to the way that the eyes, head and body move. It is in turn linked to what is stored in memory and what the person's intentions are so that 'the organism contributes to the constitution of the form' of a perception or an action (1983: 13).

If we think of an ordinary activity like putting on a pair of shoes, what Merleau-Ponty is suggesting, is that we do not apprehend the shoe as a set of individual stimuli – seeing each shoe, seeing the hole for the foot, seeing the laces, feeling each of these components first with hands and then toes and so on. What we 'see' (with our eyes and our hands and feet through which we complexly combine perceptual information) is our shoes and what we 'do' is put them on. We grasp the shoes as a form and our bodily action follows a pattern that corresponds to that form, so putting shoes on is something we can do more or less without thinking while perceptions and actions fit the form. This example shows that consciousness is only tangentially involved in the process and yet we would easily recognize that putting on the shoes is an intentional act, one which accords with our being-in-the-world and is not pre-determined. There may be moments of conscious engagement, even something we might call thought, such as choosing which shoes to wear today or looking for the left shoe which is out of sight under the bed. But even these conscious engagements, which are clearly dependent on a working in concert of mind and body, do not demand much of our powers of thought.

We tend to think of judgement as a product of reflective thought but Merleau-Ponty argues that judgement is part of perception in the flow of ordinary experience in which we make distinctions and attribute meaning. He points out that perceptual illusions occur when we attribute a particular meaning to what we perceive – we make a judgement – that in the light of later information we accept was inaccurate. To illustrate this, he uses the example of Zöllner's illusion in which the two pairs of vertical lines appear to be converging from top to bottom whereas they are in fact parallel (see Figure 5.1).

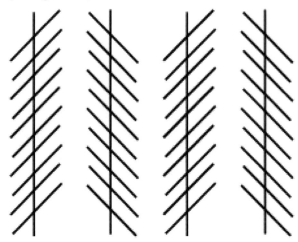

Figure 5.1 Zöllner's illusion

Our immediate perceptual judgement is that the vertical lines are converging – it is only on reflection that we realize they are, in fact, parallel. Whereas the intellectualist perspective sees this as a 'mistake', Merleau-Ponty argues that the auxiliary lines alter the meaning of the main lines as we perceive them. Before we can see them as parallel, we must first make the perceptual judgement of their relationship as converging that takes into account the meaning of the diagonal hatching: 'perception is just that act which creates at a stroke, along with the cluster of data, the meaning which unites them – indeed which not only discovers the meaning *which they have*, but moreover sees to it *that they have a meaning'* (Merleau-Ponty 1962: 36). But Merleau-Ponty goes further, to argue that even reflective judgement which appears to be nothing but a cognitive act, depends on memories of previous perceptual experience and memories of ideas, including those from the community of thinkers. Memory brings into play not only judgement entailed in perception but also judgement in terms of the truth, or not, of an idea. The operation of judgement is always situated in a particular body with its particular experiences and even analytical reflection cannot cut it off from those experiences.

Instead of the mentalist view of perception operating through the senses to generate an 'objective' picture, Merleau-Ponty describes looking at an object as being 'to inhabit it, and from this habitation to grasp all things in terms of the aspect which they present to it' (1962: 68). He is referring to the capacity to see the front of an object and be able to imagine it from various angles and retain its image, even when it is obscured by other objects, based on what we already know of objects and the field.[14] This extends to the continuity of objects in peripheral vision that remain 'dormant, while, however, not ceasing to be there' (Merleau-Ponty 1962: 68) and provides a series of 'horizons' that orient the viewer and constitute the perspective by which the phenomenal field gains structure. Merleau-Ponty argues that perception 'as seen from the inside', that is as we experience it, is a 're-creation or re-constitution of the world at every moment' and cannot be grasped as a causal process of stimulation from outside, acting on a discrete system within the body (1962: 207). His holistic account of perception understands sight as integrated and inseparable from the flow of life within the body in which perceiving and thinking are intertwined with the operation of the senses and the experience of culture.[15] What is perceived is 'intentional' because it is already caught up in the rhythm of existence through which we come into relations with external beings. The quality of being that inhabits materiality and objects within a field Merleau-Ponty describes with physiological metaphors; the body is 'geared' to the world, 'anchored' to it or able to 'grip' it (1962: 253).

This embodied engagement enables both perception and motor activity; I am geared to the world when I have a clear perception of the field and when my motor intentions can be realized within that field. The sharpness of perception and action is important because it must be sufficient to provide a 'perceptual *ground'* and so a basis for life in which being is 'synonymous with being situated ... and oriented' (Merleau-Ponty 1962: 250). The field of perception is constituted in space but also intertwined with time to provide a 'field of presence'.[16]

> There is, therefore, another subject beneath me, for whom a world exists before I am here, and who marks out my place in it. This captive or natural spirit is my body, not that momentary body

which is the instrument of my personal choices and which fastens upon this or that world, but the system of anonymous 'functions' which draw every particular focus into a general project.

(Merleau-Ponty 1962: 254)

The 'subject beneath' is the body that is familiar with the material world, that contains knowledge gained through cultural experience of how things work; it is this embodied subject that knows how to respond to the world of objects, knows how much force to apply, what the significance of visual and tactile information is. Perception depends on prior experience which is both cultural and material to make meaning of what is present in a current field. Merleau-Ponty discusses the difficulty of recognizing faces and their expressions when they are seen from upside down – we take it as 'natural' that faces are the 'right way up' because that is how we have usually encountered them (1962: 252).

Habit and embodied knowledge

Our knowledge of the world emerges through our bodily engagement with it. Although Merleau-Ponty is critical of the behaviourist account of reflexes as mechanistic responses to stimuli, he understands the reflex as a pre-conscious way in which the body orients itself to the world and the objects within it. Reflexes situate my body as a being-in-the-world in a way that I take for granted and may not give thought to:

The reflex, in so far as it opens itself up to the meaning of a situation, and perception; in so far as it does not first of all posit an object of knowledge and is an intention of our whole being, [is a] modalit[y] of a *pre-objective view* which is what we call being-in-the-world.

(Merleau-Ponty 1962: 79)

What responds to stimuli to give them meaning is my body which determines my responses in accord with its 'aims in the world', its 'possible operations' and 'the scope of our life'. It is the continuity and consistency of my bodily being in the world that are prior to specific stimuli and enable me to ascribe them meaning. This embodied sense of what it can do Merleau-Ponty calls the 'habit-body' and distinguishes it from the 'body at this moment', the experience of current actions (1962: 82). The habit-body is the taken for granted sense of embodiment with which we enter each new moment but it is vulnerable to being altered by the experiences of that moment. This is not for Merleau-Ponty a double mode of being-in-the-world since there is a flow between these two layers of embodied being; the experiences of 'body at this moment' become progressively integrated into the habit-body in which the past is always available as part of the present. As Merleau-Ponty sums it up: 'the ambiguity of being-in-the-world is translated by that of the body, and this is understood through that of time' (1962: 85).

Habits and skills, including those that utilize objects, are acquired in this cumulative way within the 'habit-body' and so are available for action in the current moment and for making sense of what is present in the field – it is 'a grasping of a significance, but it is the motor grasping of a motor significance' (Merleau-Ponty 1962: 143). The examples that he gives are of a woman who wears a feather in her hat but keeps a safe distance from things that might break it off, the car driver who can enter a narrow opening without checking the width just like someone walking through a doorway,[17] and the blind man whose stick is used to extend the scope and radius of his touch: 'To get used to a hat, car or stick is to be transplanted into them, or conversely, to incorporate them into the bulk of our own body. Habit expresses our power of dilating our being-in-the-world, or changing our existence by appropriating fresh instruments' (Merleau-Ponty 1962: 143).

This conception of habit recognizes that it is a largely unconscious process but that it nonetheless involves knowledge that has been taken into the body. It is an extension of that type of knowledge that we already have about our bodies – position, strength, possible movements, the consequence of actions for the body – that we do not have to think about. Knowledge of my body can be subjected to thought and to reflection and 'extending' it with a tool will undoubtedly require consciously reviewing what the information received 'means', as when someone newly blind learns to use a stick. What it means for the use of such an object to become a 'habit' is that the user no longer needs to interpret the pressures on the stick but simply perceives through it; 'It is a bodily auxiliary, an extension of the bodily synthesis' (Merleau-Ponty 1962: 152).

Whereas Gibson sees an object such as a hammer having the 'affordance' of hammering (see Chapter 4), for Merleau-Ponty the object must first be assimilated within the actions and intentions of the body. This may involve watching others or taking advice and it may involve practice and experiment. If I am learning to use a hammer for the first time, once I have found how to grip and lift it, I need to work out how to direct it forcefully at the nail head utilizing the particular properties of the hammer (the distribution of its weight, the lever effect of its handle). For the joiner who uses the same hammer daily, this learning process is in the past and like the hat-feather wearer, car driver and blind-stick user, the hammer is not the focus of perception or of conscious thought; perception is of the nail that is hammered, not the hammer that is wielded. The habitual use of the object means that knowledge about how to use it, including what its effects are likely to be, are taken into the body and, in use, the object becomes effectively part of its user. Recalling the example of the typewriter, Merleau-Ponty says that 'the subject who learns to type incorporates the key-bank space into his bodily space' (1962: 145).

David Sudnow's (2001) detailed account of learning to play jazz piano describes the stages of acquiring the embodied skill to produce on a keyboard, the music he had previously enjoyed listening to. He had to acquire an abstract understanding of the harmonic and melodic possibilities of chords and tunes through being shown by a teacher and through transcribing from records. Along with this theoretical understanding he had to acquire two types of bodily facility. First, his hands had to be able to produce on demand the full range of chord shapes and melodic runs which meant learning the positions and sequence of fingers and how to make smooth transitions from one hand to the other or from little finger to thumb and vice versa. This kind of physical training, a sort of fitness for the hands, meant instilling the movements into the habit-body by repetition. What began with his mind controlling the operations of his fingers progressively became habitual so that he could play the various scales in any key, moving smoothly between one and the other without thinking. Second, his ear had to become attuned to the harmonic possibilities that a particular chord sequence opened up; the chord progression had to become a habit of mind so that he could hear both what was happening now and what was upcoming. These two types of bodily learning had to be put together to improvise jazz piano solos around standard tunes. The risk of such playing is the development of 'slick licks' so that a given chord triggers a particular melodic move, more or less regardless of the sequence of chords. Instead what Sudnow had to develop was a sense of the range of possible melodic moves that would work harmonically – both in the physical space of the keyboard and in the temporal space of the musical sequence – so that he was free to play and develop a personal response to the musical form, to what had gone before and to the musical situation created by the other players.

The unusual situation of a mature person determined to learn something as difficult as improvised jazz piano while reflecting on the process means that Sudnow's account is unparalleled. But everyone follows the same sort of learning process, often to a much more limited degree, many times in their lives as they learn to type on a keyboard, drive a car, cook a meal, and so on. Merleau-Ponty does not disregard the significance of reflective, conscious thought in the lives of human beings, but the effect of his philosophy is to point to how much of what is characteristically human is actually embedded in the patterned, habitual nature of everyday actions. Sudnow shows how some aspects of conscious thought have to be transformed into habitual actions of the body, so that other dimensions of consciousness can be brought into play. The example of his piano playing shows how acquiring embodied skill in the habit-body enables human beings to express themselves as distinct individuals, drawing on their culture to create something that is distinct and original. Unlike most animals, humans have very few definite instincts that direct their actions so the acquisition of embodied habits 'does at least give to our life the form of generality, and develops our personal acts into stable dispositional tendencies' (Merleau-Ponty 1962: 146). The body is a repository for patterns of actions that appear to be 'natural' or 'instinctive' but have in fact become habits, skills or 'dispositional tendencies' through being learnt from the culture.

Intentionality

It is intentionality that gives direction to perception and action in the material world while linking the material engagement of the body to its mindedness, both in the consciousness of the moment and in previously acquired habits and dispositions. In his preface to *Phenomenology of Perception*, Merleau-Ponty reminds us of Husserl's distinction between 'intentionality of act' and 'operative intentionality' (1962: xviii). Intentionality of act is where judgements are consciously applied to present situations so that, in the future, past actions can be attributed to a specific expression of will. This is what is ordinarily meant when we ask someone what their intentions were – it is anticipated that the answer will be easily forthcoming since the person's mind would have been 'made up' prior to their actions and the intentions that directed their acts would have been present in consciousness. The concept of 'operative intentionality' spreads the mindedness of intentionality to those acts of which I would not readily say 'I intended to do that' but which I nonetheless take ownership of as being mine and not the result of some alien beast working through me. This form of intentionality underlies our orientation to bodies and things in space (Merleau-Ponty 1962: 243), our very motility (Merleau-Ponty 1962: 137) and all those routine and taken-for-granted actions that we perform regularly without bringing them to consciousness. They may border on the autonomous actions of my body (the yawn that I could choose to stifle) or be activities of considerable complexity (the 10 miles I drive through a city while thinking about something completely different). Operative intentionality incorporates habits and the adoption of cultural practices and ways of doing things which are treated as 'natural' and not subject to question in the routine course of life. For Merleau-Ponty the intentions embedded in routine, habitual and ordinary behaviour produce the 'antepredicative unity of the world' (1962: xviii) – that is, it makes the world a coherent and unified environment *before* an objective stance, such as that produced by analytical thought, is taken up. It would be wrong to think of these two forms of intentionality as distinct modes of mindedness because we may move between them as the attentiveness of our consciousness is redirected;

what we intend at one time becomes a repeated action at another and a routine action at yet another time.

In making the case for his version of existentialism, Merleau-Ponty borrows the term 'intentional arc' from F. Fischer to show how behind conscious act-intentionality there is always a continuity connecting many aspects of life that are imbued with intentionality which is no longer conscious:

> the life of consciousness – cognitive life, the life of desire or perceptual life – is subtended by an 'intentional arc' which projects round about us our past, our future, our human setting, our physical, ideological and moral situation, or rather which results in our being situated in these respects. It is this intentional arc which brings about the unity of the senses, of intelligence, of sensibility and mobility.
>
> (Merleau-Ponty 1962: 136)

We can see in Sudnow's learning to improvise jazz just such an intentional arc in which the senses of sight and touch have been finely linked to the movement of his hands and arms to realize a cultural idiom – jazz improvised against standard chord sequences. The moral context is provided by those occasions for playing when the pianist must fit in with the other players, listening to their music to collectively create a performance for the audience. These occasions of performance are dependent upon the preparation that Sudnow and the other musicians had put into acquiring the embodied knowledge of how to play their instruments in this style. The setting, the instruments, the players and the cultural idiom all have intentionality embedded within them in such a way that intentionality of act can produce *this* performance through the intentional arc that links its various components.

What we find in the ordinary actions of humans that involve things, is a continuity of intention which links objects, actions and human capacities. The familiarity of the actions in what we might call a 'practice' and the readiness-to-hand of the objects make them all seem 'natural' and devoid of intentionality. But as Merleau-Ponty has it, there are 'intentional threads' that link the material entities in a practice that is routine and familiar such as the work of a tailor:

> the subject, when put in front of his scissors, needle and familiar tasks, does not need to look for his hands or his fingers, because they are not objects to be discovered in objective space: bones, muscles and nerves, but potentialities already mobilized by the perception of scissors or needle, the central end of those 'intentional threads' which link him to the objects given. It is never our objective body that we move, but our phenomenal body ... as the

potentiality of this or that part of the world, surges towards objects to be grasped and perceives them.

(Merleau-Ponty 1962: 106)

At some point 'intentionality of act' has invested each of the objects with its particular design and its placing on the workbench, just as it has been applied to acquiring the skills of using them. But intentionality has become embedded in the objects and the person so that threading them together in the flow of routine action requires little in the way of conscious act intentionality.

Even though 'operative intentionality' begins to take on the flavour of a mechanical action, (the sort of process that a machine could be assigned), conscious intentionality is always ordering the action and the objects. The hands that guide the sewing machine, the thought that goes into designing the programme which guides an automatic machine, must draw on conscious intention to focus and direct the intentionality embedded in things and bodies. Indeed, for Merleau-Ponty, conscious intentionality is what gives 'form to the stuff of experience', providing an organizing theme for future actions as it lies 'beneath the flow of impressions':

Now it is not possible to maintain that consciousness *has* this power, it *is* this power itself. As soon as there is consciousness, and in order that there may be consciousness, there must be something to be conscious of, an intentional object, and consciousness can move towards this object only to the extent that it 'derealizes' itself and throws itself into it, only if it is wholly in this reference to ... something, only if it is a pure meaning-giving act. If a being is consciousness, he must be nothing but a network of intentions.

(Merleau-Ponty 1962: 121 – ellipsis in original)

Conscious intention may initiate actions and provide an organizing 'intentional object' such as the removal of a road wheel to get access to a brake assembly. We can imagine that as the experienced garage technician performs the routine task of removing the road wheel, the conscious intention that gives his activity meaning, is 'thrown into' the actions so that his lunch or a recent conversation with a colleague occupies his thoughts. But once he moves to inspecting the brake assembly, what to do next will come to the fore in his network of intentions and be a topic for conscious reflection before any subsequent sequence of actions.

Being and things

Merleau-Ponty's account of being-in-the-world as being from the first, embodied, brings him to a similar position to Heidegger's on the presence of objects for human beings. For Heidegger, things are taken up in actions and as such they are primordially ready-to-hand; it is only in a second moment of conscious reflection when we confront them as present-at-hand that they appear as if they were complete beings in themselves. In the course of everyday life a thing appears familiar and in keeping with the setting and in that sense is 'real' in the fullness of its signification so Merleau-Ponty calls it *in-itself-for-us* (1962: 322). But if we confront the object, abstracting it from the flow of everyday life, it becomes something else, something alien and other, and we realize that perceived significance and existence, though they appear as one, are not always in fact. This is what happens when the object is measured, rendering its size, weight, distance or colour in systematic terms. However, a 'thing' can never be properly a being in-itself because knowledge of its existence is always dependent on our prior perception of it that, phenomenologically, appropriates the object in relation to the body. For example, size is tied up with the distance away that the object is perceived; a small object far away is insignificant and unrecognizeable whereas close up, under a microscope, it may be of great interest. Everything in the material world that I encounter is related to my body and in order to see an object better I will move closer to it, pick it up and move it about in my hands 'because each spectacle is what it is for me in a certain kinaesthetic situation' (Merleau-Ponty 1962: 303). While at a common-sense level we might simply claim that constancy is a property of objects in the world, what Merleau-Ponty points out is that prior to objective knowledge of the constancy of the world, our bodies *perceive* this constancy. Rather than distinguishing the different sensory information from different sensory organs we take in the thing as a whole to make sense of it. For example, colour is not seen in itself but is perceived in relation to other characteristics, such as texture and shape. Whereas the green of grass takes on many shades – according to the length of the grass, the strength of the ambient light and the reflectivity of the surface of the blades – we nonetheless recognize it all as being the green of grass.

For Merleau-Ponty our engagement with the material world involves a form of communication in which our senses 'question' things and 'things reply to them' so the sensory information from things is 'a language that teaches itself' (Merleau-Ponty 1962: 319). It is as 'things' respond by demonstrating some constancy within themselves that we perceive them as a thing; because all the parts of a car are linked together in a coherent and constant way so that they move as one, we can regard the car as a single 'thing'. As we engage with the world perceptually we enter into a form of communication with the things we encounter that identifies their specificity within a setting.[18] Of course, this perception of things as distinct entities in themselves is tied in with previous experience, of recognizing things from earlier situations.

Culture

Merleau-Ponty distinguishes between the artificial object, whose signifi-cance precedes its existence, and the natural object that is already in the world and whose existence antedates whatever significance it has. Whereas the natural quality of objects such as plants and rocks is contained through-out them in a way that is alien to humans, tools and other artificial objects 'seem to be placed on the world' and the intentionality within them is apparent to human perception. This prior human quality in the artificial object is what we recognize as its cultural origins and it is through inter-preting it within the context of culture that it takes on a specific meaning. As we perceive an artificial object we bring to it our cultural understanding so that it is 'not actually *given* in perception, it is internally taken up by us, reconstituted and experienced by us in so far as it is bound up with a world, the basic structures of which we carry with us' (Merleau-Ponty 1962: 327).

If the possibility of subjective knowledge of the world moves from cer-tainty of perception in the moment of experience to interpretation and modification through reflection, this is not the individualized process that it often sounds in Merleau-Ponty's writing. He links our subjective experi-ence of the world beyond our bodies to one shared with others through the medium of material culture:

> Not only have I a physical world, not only do I live in the midst of earth, air and water, I have around me roads, plantations, villages, streets, churches, implements, a bell, a spoon, a pipe. Each of these objects is moulded to the human action which it serves. Each one spreads round it an atmosphere of humanity which may be deter-minate in a low degree, in the case of a few footmarks in the sand, or on the other hand highly determinate, if I go into every room from top to bottom of a house recently evacuated ... The civiliza-tion in which I play my part exists for me in a self-evident way in the implements with which it provides itself.
>
> (Merleau-Ponty 1962: 347–8)

The significance of cultural objects is that I experience the presence of others within the object, even if I do not know that person – I may not even be familiar with their culture. If I unearth a spoon, it may not look quite like any spoon I've every seen and yet I can perceive it as a spoon used by another person, even though I may only guess at when it was so used, by whom and with what food. For Merleau-Ponty this connection is through a generalized 'I'; I can imagine someone else using this spoon because I can imagine using it myself. The generalization to many possible 'I's that all use spoons is through the body which I take it that the 'other' has and uses as I would my own. This, 'the body of another' which, he says, 'like my own, is not inhabited, but is an object standing before the consciousness which thinks about or constitutes it' is how we can solve 'the paradox of a consciousness seen from the outside, of a thought which has its abode in the external world' (Merleau-Ponty 1962: 349). It is because we share the structure of our bodies and, most importantly, the relationship between consciousness and the perceptual experience of our bodies, that we are able to share the world. And our sharing of the material environment of the world through the ways we adapt and modify it, is what brings about the possibility of culture as we know it.

An object that we encounter can be recognized as a thing *in-itself* but a living human body is recognized as more than that, as something existing *for-itself*. I recognize the internal link between my phenomenal body and that of the other and I recognize that it perceives the world and has an intentional orientation to it, even if it is not mine. What is more, I recognize that the other being has its own phenomenal field so I am compelled to accept that the world is no longer merely mine: 'Already the other body has ceased to be a mere fragment of the world, and become the theatre of a certain process of elaboration, and, as it were, a certain "view" of the world' (Merleau-Ponty 1962: 353). Though I know that the other is *for-itself* and as such distinct from my self and intentions, I can recognize a parallel ('a miraculous prolongation') with my intentions and a familiar way of dealing with the world. It is the materiality of our bodies as structures situated in the world, perceiving and acting in it, that provides the common ground between myself and the other person. However, the other is constituted not simply in the materiality of its own body but also by its orientation to the world around it as it 'annexes natural objects ... makes tools for itself, and projects itself ... in the shape of cultural objects' (Merleau-Ponty 1962: 354). The most important of these is of course language which gives complexity to our social world, enabling us to share in our dealings with the material world in which our experience is grounded.

Conclusion

What we get from Heidegger and Merleau-Ponty is a phenomenological perspective that situates human being in the material world prior to the world of thought, reflection and objectivity. In that material world the human being confronts the stuff of the world through its own material being and within the constraints of its form. This perspective counters the tendency to think of the material world as a product of human thought as is often the case with the critics of technology in society. There is a lived relation with materiality that is prior to the complexity of modern technology that endures despite that complexity simply because the everyday, lived world of human beings is first and foremost embodied. The phenomenological philosophers do not provide a method for studying the relationship between lived human being and the material world but they do provide a number of what, after Blumer, we might call 'sensitizing concepts' (1969a: 147). From Heidegger we get concepts that include 'dealing with', 'concern', 'circumspection', 'readiness-to-hand' and 'enframing', and from Merleau-Ponty we get concepts such as 'embodiment', 'field', 'habit', 'intentional arc' and 'operative intentionality'. What we get from Merleau-Ponty that is a definite extension of Heidegger's phenomenology is a detailed account of the process of perception that locates it not only in the body but also, and this is most important, within the culture. Merleau-Ponty explains to us how the embodied responses of the human being do not depend on the mechanical properties of the organs, such as the eyes, but on the previous experience of that being. That previous experience may be personal, direct embodied experience but it may also be generalized, cultural experience that is acquired by the individual being through the body by being taught or having 'picked it up' by observation and familiarity.

This phenomenological perspective challenges both the empiricism of James Gibson's notion of affordances and the social construction perspective that has come to be so influential in the sociology of technology. Gibson's psychology of perception moves towards phenomenology with its disavowal of cognitivism and behaviourism and its acceptance of much from the Gestalt psychologists. But Gibson ultimately wants to ground the notion of affordance in the physical properties of objects prior to their entry into the world of living beings. This produces a curious form of interpretivism that eventually has to assert what objects afford; Costall's 'canonical affordances' at least resituate them within the social realm of linguistic meaning. The moves by Costall and Hutchby to socialize the concept of affordance bring it closer to the social constructionist perspective that was in Chapter 4 exemplified by the ANT perspective. Social constructionism takes the primordial form of sociality to be communication via language, text and interpretation but this tends to omit the lived, embodied form of material engagement with the world. What I hope to have shown is that the phenomenological perspective brings together the material and communicative or cultural dimensions of social existence.

The phenomenological perspective shows us the nature of being with materiality is not fixed or predetermined but is emergent and so shaped by the temporal dimension as much as the spatial. The temporal dimension allows for cumulative experience and cultural knowledge to impact on the embodied and material experience of existence:

> The thing and the world exist only in so far as they are experienced by me or by subjects like me, since they are both the concatenation of our perspectives, yet they transcend all perspectives because this chain is temporal and incomplete. I have the impression that the

world itself lives outside me, just as absent landscapes live on beyond my visual field, and as my past was formerly lived on the earlier side of my present.

(Merleau-Ponty 1962: 333–4)

The dimension of temporality gives context and meaning to our experience of the world and the beings in it. Rather than being distinct, each perception merges into the next and so our world is continuous and uninterrupted (Merleau-Ponty 1962: 328). This continuity extends to space so that what lies beyond the field of sight or beyond the present, in the future or the past is treated as continuous. There is an indeterminacy about what is out of range of my senses that contrasts with the 'uniquely compelling reality which defines my present here and now' (Merleau-Ponty 1962: 331).

6 Material interaction

Introduction

> Objects are for us, often without our recognizing it, the com-
> panions of our actions, our emotions and our thoughts. They
> not only accompany us from the cradle to the grave. They
> precede us in the one and survive us in the other. Tomorrow
> they will speak our language. But are they not already speak-
> ing to us, and sometimes much better than with words?
>
> (Tisseron 1999: 12)[1]

Tisseron suggests that our emotional relationship with objects is tanta-
mount to us talking to them as we would a confidant ... or a psychoanalyst.
He is anticipating a world in which objects do literally 'talk', as my computer does when it suddenly declares that my 'battery is fully charged' or as
a truck does when it announces to anyone within earshot 'attention,
vehicle reversing'.[2] But this is not so subtle a form of communication as the
way objects such as motor vehicles already 'speak' to us through our
embodied interaction when we drive them. We 'read' the road (even
through the rear-view mirror when reversing) and feel the progress of the
vehicle through our senses of sight and the kinaesthetic information from
our limbs and body. The resistance of the steering wheel and the feel of
brakes through our bodies allow us as drivers to interact with the object of
the vehicle (see Dant and Martin 2001; Dant 2004). Our interaction with
the artefacts of modern life, such as motor vehicles, depends on the way
that they have been intentionally designed for use and it is the meeting of
this object embedded intentionality with our own that produces interaction with things.

As we saw in previous chapters, the idea of interaction between individuals and objects is not new; both Schiffer and Heath and his colleagues
(see Chapter 1) have developed different analytical strategies to tackle interaction with material objects and such interaction is implicit in the theories
of agency discussed in Chapter 4. There have been attempts to record the

embodied nature of action such as Birdwhistell's (1973) system for studying body-motion communication and Labanotation that can be used for 'writing' human actions (see Farnell 1994). The emphasis in these approaches is on the communicational dimension of human action and the interaction is primarily between humans sharing the same time and space and of a symbolic nature.[3] Indeed, the traditional approach to the study of material culture has been to focus on objects as signs or symbols – Barthes ([1964] 1993) and Baudrillard ([1968] 1996) provide founding instances of this approach.[4] The shortcoming of the perspective that treats material culture as symbolic representation is that it treats the specificity of the object as largely irrelevant; my car may be a sign of my social status, but then so may my watch or my suit. How these different objects fit into my everyday life is clearly quite different as is the material interaction that I have with them. They connect me to my social milieu in quite different ways even though they may all confirm my social status. The argument of this book is that material objects contribute to human cultural life in an even more fundamental way than signification, through embodied interaction with the object – a process that I have called 'material interaction'.

This chapter will draw on the 'Car Care' project to illustrate various modes of interacting with things.[5] Cars are built on production lines where the interaction between humans and objects is largely shaped by the machine tools that are used. But in the setting of maintenance and repair garages the technicians organize their work quite differently to 're-produce' the car, to return it towards the state it was in when it left the factory. This type of work lends itself to close observation because many of the objects being worked on are large enough for an observer to see and record with a video camera. The work is very much 'embodied' in the sense of requiring the whole body of the technician to be involved; most of the time, hands, eyes and mind are working together to interact with the range of material objects that are the car, its parts and the tools used. However, all the objects in a garage that the technicians interact with are artefacts designed or intended for use in particular ways – even modern engine oil is synthetic and produced to exact specifications. They are not natural objects that have to be shaped for a purpose and the technicians are not required to 'create' new objects.[6] The skill of the technicians lies in identifying how to work with the available artefacts, some of which respond as expected, others of which do not.

Interaction

An engineer who is constructing a bridge is talking to nature in the same sense that we talk to an engineer. There are stresses and strains there which he meets, and nature comes back with other responses that have to be met in another way. In his thinking he is taking the attitude of physical things. He is talking to nature and nature is replying to him.

(Mead 1962: 185)

As George Herbert Mead suggests, interaction, even with an inanimate object implies a reciprocity between the human actor and the thing. There is an asymmetry in the interaction in that, while humans have the capacities of will and intentionality, objects, in themselves, do not. Usually this means that it is the human who initiates and controls the pace of the interaction although some objects, such as those with motor or electronic capacities, can determine the pace and even the sequence. Artefacts – unlike Mead's 'nature' – have embedded within them the intentional actions of those who designed and manufactured them. This intentional quality in artefacts may be at some distance in time or space from interactions with them and it may have been modified by other intentional behaviour, for example, through a regime or devised practice that modifies original intentions. The engineer talks to nature when he builds the bridge but all those who drive over it interact with the engineer's intentions as modified by those who designed the regulation of traffic that uses the bridge.

For Mead, what is distinctive about human action is its orientation to meaning which is, he argues, generated within society so that 'objects are constituted in terms of meanings within the social process of experience' (1962: 77). It is this orientation to meaning rather than to information that makes the approach of Mead and the symbolic interactionists so different from Schiffer's concern with the communication of 'information' (see Chapter 1, pp. 6–8 above). Information can be handled by a machine but meaning requires the response of a human who has learnt from their society what things mean. For Mead and for Herbert Blumer, objects may have meanings but they are attributed by the social human being who perceives them. Mead's approach has much in common with the phenomenologists in that he recognizes that the significance of objects is not as things in themselves but as objects that are taken up in particular actions or activities. He talks of the orientation towards objects in the distance and that as they become closer they enter a 'field' of perception and eventually come into range within a manipulatory area[7] where they can be taken up for a purpose ('We organize the field with reference to what we are going to do', Mead 1962: 278). Mead, not unlike Merleau-Ponty, distinguishes a scientific account of the material world from that of a social actor who attributes meaning to it using the capacity of mind rather than systematic measurement. The importance of identifying the meanings of physical objects is that they allow the human to control them from the standpoint of her or his own responses (Mead 1962: 131–2). The attribution of meanings is a capacity of 'mind' but in Mead's account arises within social process and social interactions.

What I am calling 'material interaction' depends on the socially acquired human skills for recognizing in the form of things what can be done next with them. These skills are acquired through the culture but they are also embedded in the objects with which we deal. This means that the artefact itself embodies the intentional actions of prior human beings that are released in the interaction with the present actor. So, the size and shape of an object, say, a threaded bolt with a hexagonal head, constrain how it shall be interacted with; it becomes fixed when tightened into a matching thread on a nut or other component, is removed by overcoming static friction and turning it to the left, its head is designed to be gripped in the jaws of a spanner and it achieves the linking of one object to another (usually with other similar bolts) but has no other mechanical purpose in itself. Interaction with the bolt may discover variations in meaning; that the thread is left-handed or that the addition of a spring washer allows the fixing to move under friction, and so on. The intentional, artefactual form of the objects that go together to make a car means that they are all there for a purpose which is entailed in that of the car (to move and stop in certain ways with certain qualities of safety, comfort, speed, control, and so forth). Both the purpose of the objects and the way they contribute to the mechanical whole of the car are, more or less, embodied within the object; the technician can assume that they were intended to 'work' mechanically in specified ways.

Herbert Blumer provides a succinct account of what 'symbolic interaction' means: 'human beings in interacting with one another have to take account of what each other is doing or is about to do; they are forced to direct their own conduct or handle their situations in terms of what they take into account ... One has to *fit* one's own line of activity in some manner to the actions of others' (1969a: 8). For the symbolic interactionists, physical things are important in the context of human interaction and the meanings of objects become significant as the background or context for interactions and may contribute to the process of interactions.[8] But I wish to go further than either Mead or Blumer, to suggest that human beings interact with objects that have a social dimension beyond their symbolic meaning. I am arguing that as the social human being interacts with an object, she or he must take account of what the object is doing or is about to do and must fit their line of activity to the intentions embedded in the object. In this chapter I want to take Mead and Blumer's version of interaction but extend it to interaction between social beings and artefacts using some of the ideas and concepts of the phenomenologists, Heidegger and Merleau-Ponty, that we encountered in Chapter 5. Let me begin with undoing a nut.

In this example we find a technician – I'll call him Ray – undoing the nut on the front wheel bearing of a car. He has removed the split pin that locks the nut and he knows from experience that it is going to require considerable effort to move the nut itself. What we see is that he has a sequence of different types of 'undoing' responses to the nut's resistance. To begin with, he puts a socket together with an adjustable lever bar to form a spanner, and on the end of the lever that is part of the standard tool, he adds a length of pipe so that he can exert extra pressure.[9] Having arranged the extended lever for the movement that follows, he puts both hands on the end farthest from the nut and bears down on it, with the weight of his body pushing down through his straight arms, his knees bending as the lever moves (see Figure 6.1). This movement moves the nut no more than an eighth of a turn but he knew before he began that this embodied technique and arrangement of tools was likely to be needed to overcome the initial static friction.

Figure 6. Ray's persuader

Ray then removes the extension pipe and, kneeling down in front of the nut, he realigns the socket and lever and makes a further quarter turn using two hands to completely free the nut. He then disassembles the spanner so that an extension bar can be fitted between the socket and its lever. In its new form there is to begin with a long end and a short end of the lever bar which gives him a little less purchase while another quarter turn is made, this time with one hand on the long end of the lever and one at the hub of the socket (see Figure 6.2). Feeling that the nut is running sufficiently free, Ray then adjusts the lever bar so that each end is roughly equi-distant from the turning point and one hand on each end to turn it.

Figure 6.2 Two hands on lever bar

With the tool in this alignment the nut is worked looser, the hands working fluidly together to drive the lever-bar. At first the left hand tends towards working the lever while the right hand moves behind it to support the socket to keep the spanner aligned on the nut. The left hand drives down and round through about half a turn before it moves to pick up the other end of the lever which it similarly drives through half a turn. But as the nut becomes looser and offers less resistance, both hands work towards the centre, turning the spanner more rapidly at the same time as supporting it, without using the purchase of the lever. Then, in a final phase, the spanner is withdrawn completely and held loosely in Ray's left hand, while the right takes over turning the nut directly (see Figure 6.3). At first, there is clearly still some resistance in the nut and the whole wrist is used to exert the turning movement but as it loosens, just the fingers are able to spin the nut before it is finally removed.

Figure 6.3 Finger loosening

In this example of material interaction, Ray takes up a series of bodily techniques and arrangements of tools in response to the resistance of the nut. As the resistance reduces, he changes to an action that involves progressively less leverage but greater speed and continuity of turning movement; he interacts with the nut through his whole body via the tools, responding to its changing resistance. There is a reciprocity that is not precise or pre-planned – this is not a mechanistic response that measures or calculates resistance precisely. Ray uses techniques that he has acquired over years of practice that are appropriate to his strength and bodyweight, to the tools he has available and to the way that nuts of this size, with this thread, used in this way on cars, tend to work. In a different garage we saw different techniques to deal with nuts – different types of spanners, different angles of work – but they all followed a similar sequence of response in which the nature of an action was in response to the 'feel' of the nut through the tools.

In the smoothness of the actions of turning the nut and of moving from one technique and tool arrangement to another we can see Ray's 'habit body' acting without great thought or deliberation. This is a process of 'operative intentionality' in which conscious intention lies in the past as the series of actions were learnt or acquired as practices appropriate to this sort of situation. The techniques Ray uses are securely embedded in his body, learnt and practised over many years; his body knows how to respond to the responses of the nut perceived through the tools. In Mead's terms, this is a 'conversation of gestures' in that there is no symbolic interaction that requires conscious activity of the mind to interpret what is going on. Blumer prefers the term 'non-symbolic interaction' for this type of process that is most apparent in reflex responses when human beings 'respond immediately and unreflectively to each other's bodily movements' (1969a: 8). The continuity of intention survives through the sequence of actions that Ray follows and there is no indication that he has to think or form a conscious intention before proceeding with the next action. It is the state of the friction in the nut that tells him when to move from one undoing strategy, one configuration of tools and use of the body, to the next.

Field

In the example above we can see that Ray is working in what Merleau-Ponty would call a 'phenomenal field' in which he has located himself in such a way that he can see the work and can touch all that he needs. When he leaves the field, his place in it is visible as a point at the centre and bottom of a rough semi-circle on the floor that would be made by the sweep of his hands and in which his tools lie, and extends upwards in space at least to the top of the wheel arch (see Figure 6.4). The phenomenal field is not a defined or delimited space but is to do with perceptual range of the person's body so that as the body moves, so does the field. It is the space in which the perceptual and motor apparatus of body can operate in relation to the focus of the task. From his position facing the axle of the car Ray can see, reach and touch the tools and parts he is working with and move his body to fine tune the perceptual field.

Figure 6.4 Field

In this case, and rather unusually, Ray is working from kneeling down on an old cushion that emphasizes his place in the field of his work. The kneeling position makes the field somewhat closer and more defined than it is when a technician works standing up. Ray is replacing a worn ball-joint and the damaged rubber gaiter from around the constant-velocity joint.[10] From his kneeling position he can touch the parts and reach the tools, leaning forward on his knees to get closer (see Figure 6.5), sitting back on his heels to look at the work, reach for a tool or prepare a part. The field of activity is a perceptual field as well as a manipulatory zone; within this area he can see the objects well and judge their orientation. The tools are literally 'ready-to-hand' as they are drawn up into use and on the video recording, the metallic clang can be heard as spanners are dropped to the floor within reach during the work. There is a wander-light attached to the bodywork of the car that illuminates the field, particularly the parts of the car that he is working on in the shadow of the wheel arch and as he leans forward to focus the perceptual and manual capacity of his body on the axle end, the phenomenal field narrows as in Figure 6.5 where he is beginning to undo the nut on top of the ball-joint.

Figure 6.5 Close field

Ray's hearing extends beyond the phenomenal field of sight and touch so that he is able to hear when he is called to the telephone or when a customer comes into the garage (both of which happen during this job). But while he is working closely on the ball-joint, there are many other things within the garage that are merely present-at-hand, where it is currently of no importance whether they are within sight or not, within reach or not. Within the field of his workspace the objects are under Ray's 'circumspection' and available to be drawn up into action as the work demands. He knows the direction in which to reach to pick up a tool and his hand and body orient towards the tool before his eyes are directly focused on it. The gaze rests on the object just before his hand so that his eyes are part of the touching that becomes a picking up (the flow of these sorts of actions can be seen on video but is lost to still shots).[11] Once an object is grasped, sight is directed to where it is to be moved to rather than following the object while it is in control of the hands. As Merleau-Ponty tells us, sight is not just about the function of eyes but is always linked to the whole body. Some objects Ray looks at closely, bringing them before his eyes with his hands, as for example when cleaning a tool or part, but circumspection is part of an almost continuous orientation to the touching, picking up and manipulating of tools and parts within the phenomenal field. The car is stationed over a 'pit' and from time to time Ray gets up and descends into the pit to work from underneath and behind the wheel. In Figure 6.6 he gets into the pit to use a compressed air driver to undo the three nuts securing the ball-joint to the car. What he is doing is moving around within the workspace in which the focus is the area at the end of the axle he is working on. As he moves his head and hands closer to the work, the phenomenal field becomes smaller and when he moves down into the pit, the phenomenal field, oriented as it is to his body, is in a reversed orientation to the workspace pictured in Figures 6.4 and 6.5. Circumspection of the workspace and the tools and parts is broken while he negotiates the steps but continues from the other side of the work, taking in the same array of tools and parts, albeit from a different angle.

Figure 6.6 Field from the pit

There are moments when Ray leaves the phenomenal field of this job either to go to talk to someone in the office or to fetch a tool or part. When he leaves the phenomenal field of this job, circumspection for the work in hand is broken as his perceptual field moves with him – but when he returns, his body slots into the phenomenal field again as he takes up his position in relation to the objects he has been working with. Alfred Schutz and Thomas Luckmann distinguish between 'zones of actual reach' and 'zones of restorable reach' which emphasizes the temporal capacity of the human mind to retain features of a phenomenal field that can be recovered or restored from the person's stock of knowledge (1974: 36–8). They point out that social actors can assume the constancy of the life-world including the capacity to repeat an action in that situation – such as picking up a spanner to work on a nut. Zones of restorable reach lie outside the present moment of action, but they transcend the zone of actual reach because of the body's capacity to remember through typifications the meaningfulness of a particular situation. Schutz and Luckmann point out that while this capacity for retaining an orientation in space is to do with the human memory, zones of actual reach are shared as memories of 'a common surrounding world' so that the life-world has a social dimension (1974: 40).

As Ray fetches something for the job he is 'de-severing' the object, in Heidegger's jargon, withdrawing it from the present-at-hand, into the ongoing activity that it would have had no part in until that moment. The object – at one point he gets a small jack – is brought into the phenomenal field where it remains ready-to-hand for its part in the job. The field of the workspace develops as the work proceeds; not only are more tools drawn in but as the road wheel comes off and the ball-joint is separated and removed, that which is accessible to being seen and touched is reconstituted. Ray manages the field, dropping tools casually in it – though they don't bounce or skid out of reach – and while they are not precisely arranged they are not all on top of each other. There is a small box into which he puts the wheel nuts and the bearing nut which are removed at the beginning of the job and will be almost the last parts to be replaced on the vehicle; it is important that they do not get dispersed or hidden underneath other things. This strategy of arranging tools in use and parts that will be needed again was typical of the repair work we saw in all the garages; technicians would create a field of work with tools and parts oriented to the bit of the car they were working on. But this field would not have systematic features or prescribed limits and the arrangement of objects within it would be opportunistic or casual. Instead of a systematic ordering of parts and tools in the workspace (e.g. according to size or category or according to their physical relation within the assembly), they were clustered within the phenomenal field. As parts come off, they are left near to where they were removed and within loose groupings but because they are available for circumspection the effort of arranging them systematically is redundant. Nonetheless, their arrangement does follow the pattern of the work; a technician said, 'When I put things down I put them in groups ... things generally fall into place' (Tape 75 00:58:00:02). The end of the job was often signalled by the disassembly of the workspace as tools were returned to the tool chest and replaced parts disposed of, thereby reconstructing the field as available for a new task.

An extreme example in the corpus of data that involved dealing with removed parts was where a whole engine had been taken out and was being replaced. Many of the parts from the original assembly, including connecting components like nuts and bolts, were kept for re-use. What appeared to an outsider as chaos was not chaotic to the technicians involved. They did not follow an instruction manual in undertaking the refit and the components were not set out in space to prepare for the sequence of actions in time. However, components were clustered in space within the phenomenal field. New parts were kept separate in a cardboard box, each component still wrapped in plastic or smaller boxes. The larger removed parts were kept in a plastic bin and there was a small plastic box for smaller parts (on the right of Figure 6.7, under the technician's hand). However, the smaller parts were often spread out on the floor and mixed with sockets and other tools that had been used (as in Figure 6.7) – other small parts were left in the ledges around the top of the engine compartment.

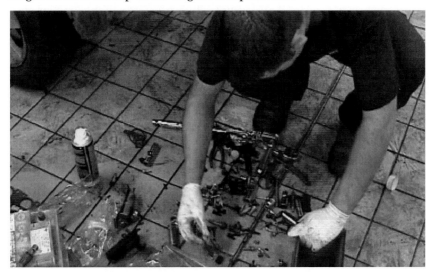

Figure 6.7 Bits for the engine refit

The two technicians working on this refit had an idea of where different sorts of things would be and knew where to look so, as a part was needed, they searched through an array of objects using eyes and fingers to identify components. Here the phenomenal field was rather larger than with Ray's work on the ball-joint. The car was on a lift and the technicians usually worked standing up – their workspace was focused around the front of the engine compartment and extended a couple of paces to either side of it. The work flowed as parts were brought to the engine and fitted – when asked if he had a mental picture by which the work was organized, Mike, the senior of the technicians said 'Not really (.) it's mainly ah (1) it's the same way as it came off really (.) got to do the easiest stuff first (.) there's so many bits and pieces which (.) which get lost otherwise' (Tape 20 01:27:13:16).[12] The work was organized by the intentionality built into the engine as holes that were intended to be filled and parts that were intended to be connected were dealt with, starting with the most inaccessible. The engine unit was first put in place and then the various linkages with the car were joined up including the various parts that had to be bolted on. Bolts for particular areas of the work were stored in different places and within those places we can see the technicians periodically sorting through to find just the size or shape of bolt or nut that was needed. As Mike picks out a bolt, he does not measure it or even read the size on it as he sometimes does when choosing a socket for his spanner. Instead he looks at it, picking it up in his fingers so that he 'inhabits' the part, understanding its meaning in relation to where it will fit in the task of reassembly.

In Heidegger's account of being-in-the-world, bringing a part or tool from the present-at-hand to being ready-to-hand means that the part sought 'withdraws' from the environment as it is identified but, as Heidegger explains, this is because of the work, the 'towards which', of the thing rather than its visible properties. In Figure 6.7 Mike's hands and eyes are looking through a collection for the part which can be taken up into the use he has in mind – the part literally withdraws from its environment of a disorganized group of parts on the floor as he picks it up. Heidegger says, 'The fact that observation is a kind of concern is just as primordial as the fact that action has *its own* kind of sight' (1962: 99). The concern in the looking is oriented to the action of refitting the engine in the car rather than, for example, sorting or categorizing the parts. Although it often appears casual and imprecise, car mechanics notice where things are put as they remove them – it is a kind of 'concern' – and the actions of their hands in disassembly and re-assembly are part of that concern and so part of that sight. Their concern is with bringing things into being ready-to-hand; this is not about making categorial distinctions or about describing or noting the world about them, and even less about scientifically measuring or understanding it.

The way in which tools and parts are distributed throughout the phenomenal field and the way that they are brought into the actions of work are recognizable as embodied action in the way that Merleau-Ponty understands it. The phenomenal body of the technician works in concert with the phenomenal field and all that is within it to bring about material interaction that is oriented towards the task in hand: replacing a ball-joint or refitting an engine. The contiguity between body and the material field is noticeable not only in the way that technicians draw tools and parts into their actions but also in the way that their bodies do not get caught on the material stuff they are dealing with. What is noticeable to a non-technician is the ease with which the habit-body of the technician moves in and around the car and the parts. They duck as they move under cars, their hands move confidently in and out of confined spaces – sometimes where they cannot see – and they do not trip or walk on parts or tools. Injuries do of course occur but in their usual workplace they are able to move and use their bodies without great care or thought because the complex material environment is so familiar as a phenomenal field.

The way in which the whole body would on occasion be used in a complex way to interact with the materiality of the field can be illustrated from the task of refitting the engine. Here the car is off the ground on a hydraulic lift and Mike has the weight of the engine supported by a mobile crane (see Figure 6.8). He also has a jack underneath the engine unit to keep it at the correct angle as he tries to line up the engine with the transmission at the back. He is using his whole body to shove the engine unit through his left hand while he peers over it to see whether it is in position, his right hand feeling down to where the flywheel is. The perceptual apparatus of his whole body is working with his hands, the crane and the jack to align the engine with the car. The 'form', in Merleau-Ponty's language, of the body working here as a whole, means that it is difficult not only to distinguish those parts of the body that are perceiving from those that are acting, but it is difficult

Figure 6.8 Moving the engine unit

to distinguish the body from the tools that, although static, it is working with. The weight of the body works against the suspended weight of the engine, the body adjusts the alignment achieved by the jack, the action involves pushing against the floor (sometimes Mike's feet slip) and towards the car raised on a lift that is itself mounted on the floor. The hands and the eyes perceive but then so does the whole body and Mike's cenethesis is critical for the task in hand.

Intentionality

As I have described work on cars so far, I have treated it as largely a set of habitual practices that realize material interaction. No doubt much of the work involves thought, consideration and reflection but while the action flows without interruption, there is little evidence of anything other than habitual action. However, things do not always go according to plan and this usually leads to a break in what Merleau-Ponty calls the 'intentional threads' that link the current activity through the intention of the human actor, via his or her tools to the objects being worked on. It is at these points that a shift between what he calls 'operative intentionality' and 'intentionality of act' becomes apparent; this is where the intentionality in the object does not match the intentionality that forms a routine sequence of actions. Once Ray had removed the old ball-joint, he picked up the new joint still in its plastic wrapper and realized that it would not fit as a replacement. There is a moment when his hands turn over the new joint, still in its plastic bag, and compares it with the one he has removed; the new one has a different configuration of bolts and would not match those on the car or the backing plate. In Figure 6.9 we can see the new part still in its plastic bag as it is dropped to

Figure 6.9 Wrong part

the floor not far from the old part with its triangular arrangement of holes that fits the matching bolts on the mounting plate just beyond it.

As he turned the new part over in his hands there was a sense of him inhabiting the part and realizing that it would not fit. Shortly after the new ball-joint is dropped, the job is interrupted while he goes to get the cordless telephone which he brings to the workspace to ring the parts supplier and discuss what is needed and when a replacement can be delivered (see Figure 6.10). The mobility of the telephone instrument means that he can discuss the parts, old and new, with them still within his perceptual field – the break in the work and the talk about it confirm the break in the intentional thread.

Figure 6.10 On the phone

The telephone transforms Ray's phenomenal field as it is suddenly extended beyond his perceptual field in both space and time. He is able to talk to someone miles away about his problem and plan actions in the future, judging how the problem can be solved and minimally disrupt the flow of his job. Characteristically of mobile phone users, he gets up from the floor and moves about, looking into space as he waits for an answer about the delivery; once he has described the mismatch of the objects, his phenomenal field is down the telephone line and into the future. The part arrived a little later in the day and he was able to continue the fitting of the ball-joint without having to abandon the job and clear up the workspace.

While much of the work proceeds routinely and habitually as technicians take up tools and employ embodied techniques with very little apparent 'intentionality of act', there are many instances of technicians stopping the flow of action and taking stock of the situation in ways that make it apparent that they are thinking about what is going on. External evidence of intentionality of act is not always certain; how can one human being know precisely what another is thinking? But behaviourally speech often indicates that there is a conscious act of the mind that adjusts intentionality in relation to what to do next – Ray's telephone call spells out what he had been thinking. When the meaning of the objects in the phenomenal field demands reflective interpretative work, this is usually indicated by a pause in the flow of action that would take the job towards its conclusion. Perceptual activity does not stop, however, and eyes, hands and body often continue to move as sufficient meaning from the array of objects is derived to enable the technician to carry on to the next task.

On the engine refit, as Mike was reassembling the soft pipe work of tubes and the harness of electrical leads, he periodically touches them and moves the leads and pipes. Although flexible, the pipes and wires are linked together in groups with specific lengths and with most of the tubes pre-shaped with fittings that indicate where they should go and how they should fit. Although the parts contain material cues about how they fit together, it is not always immediately clear to Mike just what the correct sequence of fitting is. On at least one occasion a pipe will not go through the pipe clip he has fitted, so he has to remove the clip, fit the pipe and then refit the clip around the pipe. He also makes a number of gestural moves, such as picking up a group of cables, as he does in Figure 6.11 and placing them onto the engine more or less where they should go to prefigure what the final arrangement will be. But before they are refitted they are moved out of the way again and left to dangle to give him easier access for fitting something else first.

Figure 6.11 Moving cables

Given the complexity of the job, it is remarkable on how few occasions that realignment of components is necessary. There is clearly a lot of 'minded' thought work that orients and links actions, stringing together sequences of habitual action, although it is just about impossible for an observer to know just how much conscious intentionality is being applied at any one moment. To ask the actor would be to interrupt their work and they would then have to recover what they can remember of what had been in their consciousness ... or not. It seems likely that material interaction involves a constant shifting along a continuum from fully habitual action to fully intentional action, with varying degrees of conscious intentionality of act in any given action. In the nature of material interaction its characteristic form is a continuous flow with meaning being taken up from the objects in perception more or less without interruption – the intentional arc of which Merleau-Ponty writes.

As when Ray spoke on the telephone, there are a few instances in our corpus of data where technicians were moved to speak out loud as they worked making apparent the shift from operative intentionality to an interpretive mode to anyone in hearing range. In the following example Rob, who was fitting a replacement exhaust pipe says, 'that don't line up straight away' (Tape 3 00:06:33:05) – he is speaking partly to himself and partly to the researcher and the wry comment refers not only to this pipe but how it is fitting exhaust pipes in general.[13] Then he stands away and looks at the piece and its alignment from a different angle – he is reading the array of objects that are not going together as it appeared they were designed to. At this moment the section of exhaust pipe and its bracket are 'unready to hand' and, in Heidegger's phrase, the world underneath the car 'announces itself' to Rob who is moved to utter a comment on that world. He shortly returns to adjusting the nuts on the previous section to test the range of movement of the two pieces of pipe to try to make sense of how it is meant to fit onto the car. There are clearly a few moments of conscious reflection on the meaning of the objects but it is closely followed by interpretation that involves touching and moving the objects, trying out different orientations between them.

The touchings, twistings, shakings and re-alignings of the loosely fitted pipes happen too quickly to follow without the flow of action caught on video but three moments from the action will show something of what is involved (Figures 6.12–6.14). The problem is that the bracket on the pipe needs to fit into the rubber mounting grommet on the underneath of the car – but there is a gap too wide for any amount of 'coaxing' to bridge if the pipe is to line up down the length of the car. Having twisted the pipe on in the direction he expects it to go (Figure 6.12), he stands back to look from a different angle and sees that the support bracket sticking out at right angles to the pipe (see Figure 6.13) is too short to fit into the rubber grommet mounted on the car. He then begins to adjust both the section of pipe he has just fitted and the previous section of pipe to see if there is any way that the bracket and grommet can be made to meet. There isn't – and eventually he uses the mounting bar that he took off the old exhaust pipe. The fitting of parts, especially parts such as exhaust pipes that are neither engineered finely nor fitted firmly on the car (except at the manifold outlet), requires a considerable amount of offering-up, lining-up, checking, adjusting, fiddling-with, pushing, twisting and even bending. The manipulation of objects by hand is a form of material interaction that is complex and fluid and often precedes the interactions through the medium of a tool such as a spanner assembly.

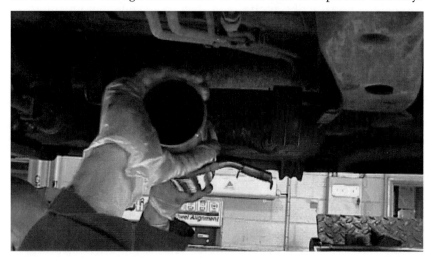

Figure 6.12 Twisting the pipe

Figure 6.13 'That don't line up straight away'

Figure 6.14 Moving the pipe

It is a frequent occurrence that as part of the continuing flow of the work, the technician will stop, touch, peer at, shake or move objects to check their state. This clearly involves an interpretative mode of interaction in which nothing is being done to transform the objects, no physical force is being applied. The interpretative mode is an interruption of the flow of intentional interaction between the human and object – it is a type of inter-action that involves consciously 'reading' the intentionality within the object array through sight and touch to prepare for the next action that will apply physical force to change the array of objects.

These two modes of material interaction – interpretative 'reading' of the objects and 'action on' the objects that applies physical force to trans-form them – may be simultaneous or they may be serial. Rob clearly paused to look and think but then he appears to continue to look and think while he touched and moved parts. The touching might have become action that would realign the pipe as part of fitting so that it would be difficult to dis-tinguish 'reading' from 'action on'. It seems likely that these two modes of material interaction, 'reading' and 'action on', are characteristic of interac-tion with most material objects. The two modes of interaction are not exactly contiguous with 'operative intentionality' and 'act intentionality' but the former is more likely to occur with 'action on' and the latter with 'reading'. The mode of 'reading' involves not only the use of sight and touch but often the whole body that moves around objects, inhabits them and alters their orientation temporarily. Sometimes tactile reading will occur through other objects such as tools and protective gloves (as with Merleau-Ponty's feather or walking stick). In the case of Rob's exhaust pipe, the components were being supported by his body and he felt the orientation of one to another through the pipes and the socket spanner he is holding in Figure 6.14.

Culture

As may already be apparent, the practices varied in different garages, even when doing the same job or same sort of job. Ray worked as a single owner/manager/technician in a garage that had equipment of a standard common some twenty or so years in the past. Mike worked in the service centre of a large dealership with up-to-the-minute equipment. These two different environments constituted different material cultures although they were both used effectively to achieve very similar material outcomes. As we have seen, Ray used a pit to gain access to the underneath of his cars, whereas in all the other garages in the study, hydraulic lifts were used to raise cars off the ground to give access underneath. The task of changing a ball-joint and a constant velocity boot were observed in other garages and were undertaken with the car raised to just over waist height on a lift so that the technician could stand rather than kneel while working. Ray's use of the 'persuader' was also distinctive; it was not a regular tool but a length of pipe that he had incorporated into his tool kit to extend the lever of his socket set. In other garages we saw equally long levers being used but they were manufactured for purpose and purchased to work with socket sets. There were a number of other differences in the way that he worked – he used a 'ball splitter', a purpose-designed tool to break the ball-joint apart whereas in another garage we saw a crowbar used for the same purpose. He also used a special tool to stretch the gaiter over the constant-velocity joint whereas elsewhere we saw the joint itself being separated before the gaiter was put on. Perhaps most distinctively Ray used two spanners together in a way that we did not see anywhere else; he inserted the jaws of one into the jaws, another to lengthen the spanner and so exert extra leverage either to finally tighten a nut (as in Figure 6.15) or to overcome static friction to get a nut moving. This was not because he did not have other tools which could have achieved the same leverage but it was a technique he had acquired and utilized over years; it meant he could work with a small, light, easy-to-use spanner and rather than change it for a different spanner could simply extend it with another spanner within reach to start loosening or finish tightening a nut.

Figure 6.15   Double spanner

The techniques of the body used in one garage varied from those in another and appeared to be determined in part by the tools and equipment available. But the techniques and experience of tool use and knowledge acquired by the technician through their career also influenced how a task was undertaken. In the dealership service centre where Mike worked, technicians were sent on courses that updated them with developments in the design and manufacture of the brand of car they mainly worked on. Within their workshop they had access to the manufacturer's specialist tools, to manuals on CDs and to a range of technicians with varying experience, training and seniority. Mike consulted a more experienced technician at one crucial point in refitting the engine and supervised a trainee technician on the same job. Ray, however, has worked alone repairing cars for many years which is a part of his being-in-the-world and an aspect of the way he approaches material interaction. The economics of running his small business do not extend to buying lots of new equipment to keep up with changes elsewhere but that does not mean that he does not have appropriate tools and techniques for the type of work he does and he is able to borrow (and lend in return) special equipment from other local garages.

The major part of repair work involves direct material interaction in which the technician uses their hands and body to work with the tools and objects that are part of the car. The phenomenal field is largely constituted by these objects which are present to the perceiving body of the technician. One of the reasons for studying closely how technicians work on cars is that it predominantly involves hand tools – spanners of a wide variety of sorts, screwdrivers, levers, pliers, grips, and so on. This demonstrates the embodied nature of the flowing, habitual practices used to respond to the intentional nature of objects – a conversation of gestures as Mead has it. But we have also seen how when things do not go smoothly, the habitual action of the body is interrupted and the mind works consciously at interpreting the meaning in the objects. I have referred to this conscious, reflective and interpretive mode of perception as 'reading' the array of objects – very different from Heidegger's 'circumspection' as objects are taken up into action.

There is, however, reading of symbolic communication that supplements the reading of the objects – textual meaning is used to enhance or facilitate material interaction. It was noticeable that manuals were rarely used to guide or organize the routine work in the repair garages but they were consulted either for checking measurements (tolerances, torque settings, volumes, and so on) or for helping out when things went wrong. When balancing tyres onto wheels, for example, they are spun on a device that calculates where and how much weight needs to be added to the rim for the wheel to roll evenly; the information is presented as a figure in a diagram on a screen that reacts precisely to sensors in the spinning mechanism. Electronic devices were also used to 'read' the state of objects; they produced symbolic information on a screen that would tell the technician precisely what measured values were. In one instance where a modern car would not start in a large dealership service centre, we observed the technician consulting a series of sources of textual information as he attempted to diagnose the fault.

Initially the technician, Roger, consults a manual kept on a CD and prints off a sheet that displays information about the electronic systems for the car. He takes the sheet to his workbench and consults it before he starts work; it contains a diagram and a list of explanations of codes. Then he moves to the car and removes the cover from the fuse box under the dashboard inside the car, where he finds a small card that is designed to tell him, again through a diagrammatic representation of symbols, what the various fuses are for and what their rating is. His eyes move backwards and forwards between the card and the array of differently coloured fuse holders according to their rating; he reads both the diagram and the array on the car (see Figure 6.16).

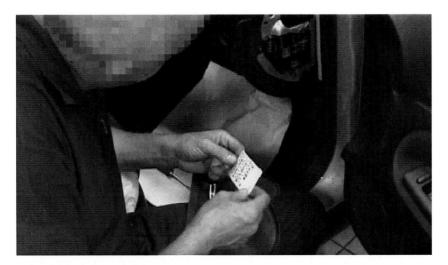

Figure 6.16 Reading the fuse card

Having replaced the fuse card in its holder he removes another piece of casing under the dash to reveal the electrical relays behind the fuses; to make sense of them, he goes to his workbench where he again consults the sheet printed out from the manual. Then he brings the sheet to the car where he can again read it and read the array of relays on the car. On the video tape we can see his head realign as his eyes move from the sheet to the car and he uses the index finger of his left hand to 'keep his place' on the relays he is reading, while his right hand holds the sheet from the manual (see Figure 6.17).

Figure 6.17 Reading a sheet from the manual

From this close reading of the car and the printout, Roger goes to an office area where he consults the full workshop manual, scanning through pages in the ring binder that include the one he has printed off from the CD. However, his next move is to fetch an electronics diagnostic test rig which is a computer with a touch-screen display on a trolley. The test rig has a cable with a multi-point plug that can be inserted into a socket in the car – the rig is mains-powered via another cable. To use the test rig, as when moving between the manual sheet and the set of relays, eyes and finger work together to find the screen he wants for this model that is headed 'vehicle self-diagnosis' with a menu for different groups of electronic functions (see Figure 6.18).

Figure 6.18 Reading the electronic test rig

The test rig reads the vehicle for him … but it fails to identify a fault. So Roger continues his own diagnostic reading of the car, going to the engine compartment where he stands for a moment looking and thinking. He then removes a cover from a group of plugs and relays; he touches these, moving them from side to side slightly, checking that they are not loose, removing one relay and one fuse, inspecting them and then replacing them. None of these readings with eyes and fingers of manuals, screens or arrays on the vehicle is successful in diagnosing the fault; it turned out to be a displaced seal that was blocking the fuel line. It was a colleague who spotted it, someone also used to diagnosing faults but not Roger who had systematically followed the electrics through from switch-on point to the engine.

Conclusion

By looking closely at how technicians interact with cars we can see something of the complexity that they take for granted in their everyday work. Kusterer (1978) refers to the practical knowledge that is displayed in a variety of types of work as 'know-how' to distinguish it from systematic or scientific knowledge and we can see that these garage technicians demonstrate that they have know-how.[14] But we can say more than this because their know-how takes a number of forms. First, at one level it is contained within the body in the sense that bodily movements are smoothly co-ordinated to achieve a particular task – such as undoing a nut – without there having to be any conscious steering of the action. Although these sorts of routine tasks involve a series of different types of action, often indicated by the use of different types of tools, the technicians move smoothly from one type of action to another within the task. These sets of actions I have treated as habitual action in that the intentionality that underlies them seems to be situated in the past, when the practice was learnt or the skill acquired. In the present, intention is merely required to set the tasks going and thereafter the process of interaction is guided by what Merleau-Ponty calls 'operative intentionality' in which there is a flowing reciprocity between the person and the objects they are interacting with – hands turning spanner, spanner turning nut, nut becoming detached from thread. But, second, even the operation of these habitual skills requires a certain level of 'intentionality of act' to be present to interpret when to shift from one type of action to another within the task – when to remove the 'persuader', when to alter the configuration of the spanner. The flow of the material action follows a pattern of reciprocity between embodied technique and the intentionality embedded in objects that cues next actions. Although the objects seem to 'call out' what is required next, the exchange between objects and human appears more or less continuous unlike the turn-taking of conversational human interaction.

However, third, we can say that 'intentionality of act ' comes to the forefront of material interaction when there is a problem that requires conscious reflection. This is what happens when the wrong part has been delivered, when the exhaust bracket does not line up or when the car won't start. On these occasions the technician moves into an interpretative or reflective mode in which his reading of the objects is interrogative, seeking to identify what has happened and what should happen. We might call this a diagnostic mode except that this would conflict with the way ordinary action is described by participants. Roger was 'diagnosing a fault' when searching electrical circuits but Ray's diagnosis that the wrong part had been sent was almost instantaneous. Rob's response to the misalignment of the exhaust bracket and grommet was in between these two types of interpretation in that despite quickly identifying a problem, he explored the nature of the problem for some time by moving, twisting and adjusting parts. Ray's diagnosis was based on reading the object; he could see that the configuration of bolt holes on the replacement part did not match that on the old part. Rob's reading of the exhaust pipe alignment involved sight and touch as he moved the parts. Roger's reading involved the sight and touch of objects (he moved relays and circuits to check for a poor connection) but it also involved reading symbolic and textual documents that in turn informed his reading of the objects.

The car technicians' work is distinctive in that it is precisely about interacting with objects unlike those people whose worklives are primarily about communicating through talk or writing. But unlike most people who create objects in factories, the car technicians undertake work at a pace and in a manner that they have control of and much of their work involves hand tools and a wide range of embodied perceptual and motor skills. Their work is not determined by a closely designed and planned production line in which every work activity is prescribed and timed – although increasingly their work is being penetrated by new technology that removes their diagnostic skills and dictates what and when their actions should be. Even so, the majority of their work requires a blend of judgement about the state of an array of objects and embodied skills with which their actions can alter the state of the objects.

Although much of the embodied capacity to interact with objects is animal in origin, we have seen how the complexity of dealing with objects requires a cultural context of acquired techniques in reading and responding to the intentions embedded in them. The skills demonstrated by car repair technicians are learnt from parents and through play as well as from formal training and watching other colleagues as they interact with objects. Institutions such as training centres, government organizations and the garage's management guide the cultural acquisition and application of specific skills. The garages we studied all operated within general safety guidelines and industry standards and those that were part of larger organizations followed advice and guidance from their parent organizations. All the garage technicians made use of manufacturers' guidance, both in relation to the cars they worked on and tools, equipment and spare parts. Both the learnt skills and the proscriptions of institutions are oriented to responding to the intentionality embedded in the physical form of the objects themselves. The meanings that technicians were able to attribute to the objects that they worked with were derived from their culture – we would expect them to be different in different situations as they were between garages and technicians with different experiences (for an extreme contrast, see Verrips and Meyer 2001).

The work of the car repair technicians is interesting because it is so resistant to substitution by machines. The original manufacture of cars (and of course spare parts) led the way, during the twentieth century, to the devising of mechanical substitutes for human skill and effort in making things. But the range of tasks involved, and particularly the wide range of objects that must be interacted with, means that the repair of machines of all sorts almost always continues to rely on human-object material interaction (see also Orr 1996). The wide range of objects involved also means that there is a high possibility of mismatch between them, as with the example of the part that does not fit or does not work as intended with other components. It is the need to cope with this wide range of possible material situations that requires the modifiable intentionality of the human to be a guiding element in the interaction between all the material entities. The embodied capacity of the human, able to adapt physically, in mode of intentionality and with creative imagination to the material situation as it unfolds, is characterized by this type of work. The technicians demonstrate the human ability to take up a wide range of tools (including hand tools, machine tools and electronic devices) in ordinary workaday uses. Although much is well practised and repetitive, car repair work also shows the variations in cultural specificity and individual ingenuity that are brought to material interactions of all sorts. This why car repair work, albeit in an intensified and sustained form, exemplifies the nature of human interaction with material objects and demonstrates the routine interface between human beings and technology and between human beings and their material culture.

This is very much how all of us deal with objects as in everyday life; we look at, handle and use them, although the interactions will tend to be briefer and involve less complex procedures. Whether putting paper in a filing cabinet, loading a dishwasher, emptying a shopping bag, driving a car or programming a video recorder, we are engaging bodily with the objects that we live with. In pre-modern cultures, engagement with the material environment would have involved much more interaction with the natural, living forms of plants and animals, of the land and things derived directly from the environment. But in late modern cultures, the material environment is predominantly artificial and increasingly technical, requiring that we interact with more complex objects in ways that follow patterns that have been intentionally built into them. We grow up learning patterns of material interaction appropriate to our culture, just as we learn to speak the language that surrounds us. Reading objects, anticipating how they will respond and acting with objects in an artificial material environment are characteristic of how we engage with material culture in late modernity.

Materiality and society

Introduction

To be human is to live in a material world in which our experience is always grounded in the actions of our bodies in relation to other material entities within our world. One of the features of human societies is that they create material entities and engage with the material world in ways that are far more sophisticated and complex than those of other animal species. As material civilization has progressed, so has the material environment which human beings have created for themselves. The human capacity to engage with the world in ways that shape the material environment must have its foundation in the embodied characteristics of the species; the particular arrangement and orientation of senses, especially sight and touch, the motor capacity of fingers, hands and limbs, and, perhaps most importantly, the capacity of mind that imagines, anticipates and communicates. These biological characteristics have enabled human interaction with the material world but it is the social arrangements of human beings that have both created the material world in which we live and have developed particular ways of acting in that world.

The social sciences have by and large tended to regard the material world as a matter for the physical sciences to be concerned with and have focused their attention on the immaterial features of cultures and societies. This has included studying the symbolic meanings of the material world when it becomes a vehicle of signs that are recognizable independent of their substantive, material form – these are the quasi-linguistic meanings of objects that can be 'decoded' within a semiological system. But what has tended to be overlooked are the more intimate and embodied relationships with objects that communicate the culture through practices that are mean-ingful to those who participate in them. What I have called 'material inter-action' responds to the intentional form of artefacts in following a cultural practice. In Chapter 6 I looked at some of the features of the interactive cul-tural practices to be found in a repair garage. Here we can see learnt and embodied techniques being used to work with a range of specific artefacts within a cultural idiom; the technicians are familiar with the way the objects around them are designed and manufactured and their embodied techniques are appropriate to them. This type of material interaction is not only characteristic of work situations such as the garage, but is characteristic of everyday interaction with material objects in the culture at large. The activities of domestic living, of moving about the society, of communicating and of interacting with other human beings also involve interaction with material objects in very similar ways; they depend on culturally acquired skills that are manifested in particular embodied practices to realize human intentions through the use of objects. There is an idiomatic relationship between series of objects and bodily practices so that the practices can respond to and realize the intentions in the objects. For example, the types of tools and the ways of using them vary somewhat from garage to garage although the ease with which trained technicians move from one setting to another suggests that this requires more of a shift in accent than of idiom. However, the embodied techniques appropriate to sewing are within a different idiom from those appropriate to driving a car and different again from those appropriate to replacing the ball-joints on a modern car. The idioms of material interaction vary over time and from place to place but, most importantly, they vary according to the types of objects involved.

We interact with material objects at work and at home, at rest and at play; the knives and forks that in western culture are part of eating many meals shape our interaction with the food we are bringing to our bodies and so affect our behaviour. How the implements are used in conjunction combined with the learnt practices of personal table manners, will provide a material context for the social interaction between us and whoever else is at the table. Using cutlery that is differently shaped or weighted from that which is familiar will remind us that we are not at home and can add an emotional quality to our interaction with the objects of the meal. The teaching of table manners and the acquisition and maintenance of cutlery are things undertaken usually within the household but both are connected through our broader social contacts to sensibilities of distinction and stratification. Experiences outside the home, at school, at the homes of others, in public restaurants and cafés, will alter and amend our behaviour and attitudes. It may only be in these contexts that we encounter sets of cutlery for different courses, (fish knives and dessert forks, grapefruit spoons or steak knives) and so have to acquire new techniques. Confronted with a pear with its skin on, or the fish with bones, we will have to adapt our practised techniques and find new ones to suit the occasion. And there will be occasions when, although used to cutlery, we will have to negotiate dealing with food directly with our hands – to eat the sandwich or the hamburger – while avoiding contaminating our fingers and clothes with loose food. In some cultures of course, eating with fingers or bread or chopsticks would be the standard culturally acquired bodily technique and would lead to a different idiom of material interaction for eating meals.

In Chapter 2, we saw that while the predominant interest of social theory has been in the patterns of relationship between human beings that constitute society, there is some recognition of the impact of the relationship with the material world on how societies take on particular forms. In exploring the idea of material civilization we saw that Marx's analysis of the changes from handicraft to industrial production were attentive to the impact of changes in material culture on the social life of people. A similar theme underlies Veblen's analysis of the 'instinct of workmanship'; in both Marx and Veblen we find an account of the emergence of modern societies with distinctive patterns of economic and social relationships that are linked to the shift from the handicraft manufacture of goods to machine-based production. The development of machine technology is itself a product of society in which ideas about the nature of the material world and the possible ways that it can be manipulated are shared between members of the society who are otherwise unconnected. As an account of material civilization, however, the tradition of social theory has been reticent in exploring how changes in the material world affect human societies beyond the process of production. There are suggestive remarks in Simmel's writing about modernity and in Veblen's recognition of the significance of materiality in marking social distinctions but it was to the historical perspective of Braudel that I turned for a recognition of the significance of materiality in the everyday lives of people. The accounts of Braudel and other historians of everyday life provide clues about the dramatic transformation in the practices and activities of ordinary existence that came about during the nineteenth century as a result of the changes to the material context in which people in industrialized countries live.

In Chapter 3 we followed some of the concerns about the nature of this relationship between technology and society that have emerged since the transformation of societies through industrialization and mechanization. There is a fear that machines could take over; their importance in the life of modern societies has become so great and their ramifications have now extended beyond the comprehension of any single individual so that they seem to be potentially overwhelming. And yet while machines take on greater levels of autonomy and become increasingly complex, they have nonetheless remained subordinate to the collective will of the members of a society. In Chapter 4 the relationship between artefacts and people as individuals within a social context was explored to see how it might best be understood. As objects take on more significance in individual and social lives, it is difficult not to think of them as having some form of independent agency. But unlike other animals or animist spirits, artefacts are only invested with agency through humans who make, modify or draw them into social actions. The meaning of objects is not simply in what they signify but in what they do or how they alter what humans do. Culture is mediated not simply through messages in linguistic or quasi-linguistic forms but is also distributed through the artefacts that shape the actions of everyone in late modern societies.

To try to unravel at a rather deeper level the relationship between human being and material entities in Chapter 5 I explored the work of the phenomenological philosophers Heidegger and Merleau-Ponty who recognize that the essence of being-in-the-world is first and foremost an embodied and material being. The contents of our experience are not exclusively physical but there is always a physical and material context for human existence. Our engagement with that material context is as a result embodied and material in itself; we engage with the world through our bodies. The perceptual apparatus that we utilize is not simply biological but is shaped by our experience, including our cultural experience, and the material world with which we interact is also shaped by the culture. Although we interact with that material world on a routine, taken-for-granted basis, this serves to obscure the impact that the culture at large has had in shaping just what that world is and how it works with our bodies.

Some of these themes were exposed to empirical and concrete exploration in Chapter 6 when I examined some of the processes involved in material interaction – the engagement of human bodies with artefacts. Here we saw how tools can enhance the motor and perceptual capacities of humans as technicians used series of tools to undertake routine repairs. The habits of their bodies were attuned to the tools and to the objects that they were working on; for them, this material world was a familiar culture in which the ways in which objects would respond was largely predictable. There are occasions when the designed and made capacities of objects did not fulfil expectations and the technicians had to resort to techniques of reflective consciousness to work out how to proceed next. Even when most demanding of mind, the relationship between human and object was physically interactive involving trial and error, adjustment and re-orientation of objects. This showed how handcraft is still central within a machine-oriented industrialized world. Power tools were used by the technicians to take the burden of physical effort out of their actions but unlike the impact of machine tools on the industrial workforce that Marx described, within the modern repair garage the individual human continues to locate and guide the tools. The interaction between humans and artefacts in the garages was in a work context but the principles of habituated routine actions, shaped by the way that the objects had been shaped, are characteristic of human interaction with objects in everyday life within and beyond work.

But there were departures from the model of human–object interaction suggested by thinking of them in terms of handcrafts, workmanship, skill and so on. Within the work, textual devices substituted for the knowledge and memory of the body and electronic devices intervened in communicating and information gathering. Electronic test equipment 'reads' the detailed state of physical objects and, in some instances, obviates the complex embodied skill of judging their state. The telephone, combined with computer database equipment, enables the flow of work and objects such as spare parts to and from the workshop. The light touch of the technician's finger on a screen, eerily reminiscent of Michaelangelo's 'Creation of Adam', brings to life a different mode of material interaction. The phenomenological engagement of the body with the material world is extended with these devices beyond the time and place of the technician, the tools and the car being worked on (see Chapter 6, Figures 6.10 and 6.18).

Design and intention

I have suggested that intentions are 'designed' into objects and this would suggest that designers have a particularly important role in shaping material culture. But while they may on occasion innovate and shape cultural practices, design is in general far more likely to reflect the contemporary culture, picking up aesthetic ideas, current styles and tendencies within material culture. Harvey Molotch (2003) has recently cast a sociological eye over the institutions and influences on the design process in modern societies; the effect of his work is to undermine any idea that individuals intentionally create material objects to have specific effects. Rather than trace intentionality back to the designer, it would be more appropriate to recognize the influence of corporate interests that produce design briefs, the consumer studies that identify a 'need' as well as the aesthetic and style influences from art, design history and contemporary trends. Designers are themselves immersed within the culture from which they learn their skills and develop their ideas and it is perhaps better to see them as the mediators of the culture in the way that Herbert Blumer suggested with his argument that the fashion elite express a 'collective taste' (1969b). He argued that the network of designers, producers, commentators and buyers of fashion were expressing a cultural tendency, catching an emerging sensibility of aesthetics and desire, rather than forming it.

The institutional nature of fashion design that Blumer identified, in contrast to the early commentators on fashion like Simmel (1971b) and Veblen (1964a), suggests that feedback mechanisms have emerged within this sphere of society that sense cultural change including the desire for more change. During the twentieth century design, the intentional creation of form in material objects, has, however, changed. More objects are likely to be 'designed' rather than simply shaped in manufacture as their form and structure are specified in a prior and separate process. The handcraft tradition meant that design was a part of manufacture and often responsive to the specific situation and end user (couture, tailoring, coach building, windows and wood panelling in buildings). During the twentieth century design became progressively standardized and separated from its specific application (for example, the 'designer suit', pre-formed double glazing – see Forty 1990 on standardization). Partly through the introduction of machine-based tools that have obviated handcraft skills, manufacture has been separated from use to follow the instrumental logic of standardization (see Forty 1990). But this has in turn led to attempts to reconnect design with use as consumer research and machine tools that can adapt to specific and personalized specifications have been developed.

The feedback between design and use has extended beyond the individual user to take in the wider effects of unintended consequences in design. Nigel Whiteley (1993) for example, argues forcefully against the dominant 'consumer-led' design agenda and for a green, responsible, ethical and feminist agenda that looks beyond the isolated relationship between an object and its user. One of the resources that Whiteley draws on is the responsive consumer who challenges design on social and ethical grounds to generate a critical perspective. A similarly critical perspective inspires Elizabeth Shove's (2003) overview of the co-evolution of cultural habits, technical systems and the material objects all of which are involved in air-conditioning systems, domestic laundry and modern bathrooms. But what she finds is an inevitability of increasingly wasteful consumption as technical possibilities are exploited in the name of personal convenience and comfort. Rather than adopting the ideology of the green consumer, Shove attempts to identify a reversing effect on the co-evolution spiral by challenging the values behind it; 'effort should focus on what it *means* to be clean and comfortable' (2003: 198 – emphasis added). She is arguing that the solution to wasteful consumption does not lie in directives to designers or invocations to consumers but in a wholesale questioning of cultural values that unpacks the intentions embedded in the artefacts, systems and practices of everyday life.

The state of material civilization has become a topic of popular culture as we try to counterbalance the separation of intentionality in the manufacture of objects and our use of them. Magazines and television encourage us to rediscover domestic skills of cooking and cleaning, and handcraft skills such as DIY, gardening and decoration. We are taught through these media – or more precisely re-taught – how to re-shape our bodies, revise our choice of clothing and re-cover lost fitness. The material world of our everyday lives is, by and large, taken for granted as we move through it but our culture is increasingly attentive to the significance that material interaction has on our lives as well as on the material world we inhabit. It is, however, professional areas of material interaction that are most likely to change the material qualities of our lives. In the sphere of medicine, genetic engineering, advances in keyhole surgery, biogenics and nanotechnology are opening up previously unimaginable transformations in everyday material lives.

Reducing illness and disability for the bodies of individuals is already the most significant transformation in material civilization over the last hundred years – the future holds even more possibilities. Material interaction depends on bodily capacities so that any reduction of impairment is an increase in the capacity for material interaction. The same principle holds true for the second most significant transformation in material civilization during the last hundred years which is the transformation of the means of warfare and violence. The ways of bringing death and injury to other people have been extended and been refined so that some countries have 'weapons of mass destruction' that they fear so much that they try to dissuade other countries from acquiring them. Giving up such weapons is not seen as a powerful bargaining tool, so lesser 'field' weapons are deployed to ensure compliance. These are largely useless against the political activist who resorts to making their own bodies into a weapon to maim and kill, often without discriminating between enemy, ally or bystander. The intentionality behind the suicide bomb is palpable but the intentions are often unclear and the unintended consequences overlooked in the fervour of what we must understand as despair.

Material civilization in late modernity

All human societies are material societies in that the artefacts produced within a culture shape and are shaped by the social actions within that culture. But since the industrial revolution, material civilization has developed apace. The workshop model of human/object interaction remains; in the garages we see human bodies working on objects to change them, often using tools as intermediaries to facilitate that transformation. But while this model persists both in our everyday lives and in some aspects of productive work within late capitalism, it is undergoing radical changes. For many people the complexity of the cultural intentions embedded within the object is not revealed to the person interacting with it. This is what the actor-network theorists would refer to as a 'black-box' scenario in which the workings of objects or a network are unavailable to those who use them. The object has the capacity to transcend the human user's own embodied materiality but in ways that can be quite mysterious. This is often what is meant by the word 'machine' in which the object takes on some human capacities without requiring its user to understand how. Such objects are not new; the camera, the telegraph, the telephone, the train, the motor car, the aeroplane, all transformed human perceptual and motor capacities in the realm of ordinary life to extend the range of transformations of human action. But the communication and informational devices of the electronic age – the telephone and the computer as interconnected networked systems – have interposed in material life to produce a further transformatory impact. Even in the workshop of the modern garage such devices extend the field of material interaction beyond the directly embodied field as we saw with the telephone and the touch-screen computer.

There are then a series of transformations of the embodied state of material interaction that have developed in late modern material civilization that extend the sphere of material interaction and its social impact.

An increase in the number of objects with which we interact

In the western industrialized world we have more interactions with increasingly different types of objects. The scenes of our domestic life – the kitchen, the living room, the study – have more and varied types of objects as we add new technologies to ancient ones. Alongside the traditional implements of pens, writing paper and the sketching pad, we can add cameras, computers and printers. Books, toys and newspapers do not disappear as we add televisions, DVD players, video games and other entertainment systems. The mixing bowl, the cooker and the chopping board are not made redundant as they are joined in the kitchen by food processors, micro-wave ovens and a myriad of other devices. Many of the items of equipment are serially acquired; cars for each member of the household; radios and telephones for each room.

Our culture is fascinated by the old as well as the new so we hoard mementoes of the past lives of our families and acquire antique or merely old objects to furnish and decorate our homes. What was once 'rubbish' (Thompson 1979) is recycled, not so much to avoid waste as to maintain continuity with our cultural past. Museums and collections gather and organize the history of our material civilization, enabling us to marvel at how far we have come; the equipment of just a generation ago has become outmoded and of interest because of its contrast with what we use now.

The objects are more complex

Both individual items and systems become more 'machinic' and the likelihood of the user knowing how they work reduces as functionality increases.[1] Electrical and electronic components increase motor and memory capacity in individual objects and timers, regulators and feedback loops control systems within objects and within our enclosed environments. In my kitchen there are digital clocks integrated into control systems in the micro-wave, the regular oven and the radio. The central heating or alarm system in an office will have timing and regulating sensors which respond to environmental shifts. The interaction between individual objects such as the telephone, the computer and the washing machine are interconnected with systems – electricity, communication, fresh and waste water – beyond the home or workplace where they operate.[2]

Yet still the automatic and independent function of these systems does not replace the traditional manipulation of material objects as we continue to burn wood, send letters and collect rain water for the garden which we distribute with a watering can. The types of material interaction with the new complex objects is generally limited – the touch of a finger on a button still requires hand and eye co-ordination but the reading of digital or textual information has become of greater significance. Negotiating drop-down menus or sequences of buttons that we must learn has increasingly replaced the more manual interaction with traditional tools and devices. Intention is embedded as functionality within the device and is less available to being adapted or variably interpreted by the user.

The range of materials has increased

The twentieth century saw the most dramatic developments in new types of plastic materials that progressively brought a massive increase in the range of durability, touch, tensile quality and colours to mouldings of all sorts. Not only are the bristles of my toothbrush of different colours and frictional effects, the handle incorporates different plastic materials for strength, flexibility and graspability. Metal alloys (stainless steel, aluminium, titanium) have been developed to compete with plastics for lightness, strength and durability. A metal casing (for a computer, say, or a camera) continues to signify the strength and durability that early plastic mouldings did not have and other materials also retain their traditional qualities, both aesthetic and physical. Wood in all its varieties is still a popular medium for artefacts, including those with structural demands like the roofs of houses. Glass and ceramics continue to be popular media in both traditional and new forms.

Objects as an interface between humans

Clothes and adornment have acted as an interface between humans probably as long as human cultures have existed and writing as a material means of communication for millennia. But by the end of the second millennium the telephone and the Internet-connected computer had established new modes of interface and interaction. The mobile video phone summarizes the confusion of embodied presence through image and talk with physical absence that characterizes much human interaction in contemporary culture. The distanciation of time and space through electronic media is changing the nature of material interaction with narrowly directed visual contact and minimal tactility. The limitations of such devices, however, remind us that at its fullest, human interaction is not simply about communication but is itself an embodied material interaction of touch and co-action such as cooking and eating a meal together.

Objects as substitutes for humans

Latour's concept of 'delegation' points to how tasks that we might delegate to a human can be delegated instead to objects like the automatic door closer (see Chapter 4). Such substitution of human action has become a feature of material civilization in the industrialized world. Men with picks and shovels are replaced by a mechanical digger, women and men with dishcloths and tea-towels by the industrial dishwasher in a hospital. Some objects substitute for the capacity or effort of the individual (spectacles, the electrical wheelchair, the automatic door) – capacities that another human might have substituted for.

During the twentieth century we became familiar with the 'labour-saving device' that substitutes for human effort, strength and manual skill but in the twenty-first century we are seeing increasing substitution of humans and interaction by communication systems (e.g. the menu system for information via telephones, Internet pages to find information and buying goods and services). Behind such substitutes there lies human intention in the design of the machine or system or in the making of certain decisions as it is operated, but the intentions become embedded within the 'system', making it more difficult to challenge. Even so, the substitution is not yet so complete as to enable automatic agents to make decisions or exercise final judgements in the way that was feared by some critics of technology and science fiction writers. Most substitutions have replaced human roles that, while they had the status of employment, no one would regard as appealing – who chooses to be a doorman?

More low-level maintenance of objects

Substitute objects are very good at replacing certain types of human actions – such as making cars or calculating the payroll – but are not so good at other types of actions such as repairing cars or gathering the data that makes up the payroll. As Marx warned, employers will substitute for skilled employees wherever they can to reduce the market value of the skill. But some less skilled jobs are not so easy to replace because they rely on such a complex range of intentional movements or perceptions that need to be finely tuned to the situation. The most characteristic of these is cleaning and the more objects there are, the more things there are that need to be cleaned and, until nanotechnology changes the susceptibility of surfaces to become contaminated, there will be many cleaning and maintenance tasks associated with the materiality of society.

More objects are both cultural and practical

The application of design has brought more and more objects to be cultural artefacts that symbolize the current state of fashion and taste while at the same time being practical objects that facilitate human actions. The car is an example of such an object that during the twentieth century became increasingly subject to design, both in its aesthetic and sensual appeal and in its ability to realize the functional requirements of a mobility device (Gartman 1994). The range of objects that can fulfil a role in our everyday lives is now so extensive that we can choose on cultural grounds rather than simply choosing the tool for the job. One of the reasons for studying material interaction within car repair garages is that decisions about form are determined by function (the alignment of holes must be right for the spare part to fit). However, in many material interactions we can choose the object for the purpose on aesthetic and cultural grounds: the kitchen spice grinder may be electrically powered and of modern design, it may be a hand-powered traditional design bought on holiday abroad, or it may be a contemporary pestle and mortar echoing the standard, almost ubiquitous, design from a couple of centuries ago.

Conclusion – material society

What Braudel noticed was that civilization is characterized as much by the material relations that enable the flow of everyday life as by the political relations that distribute resources and determine life chances. The resources and the life chances are ultimately realized in material existence. And the manifestation of material civilization is in the embodied relations between human beings and the objects they live with. The relations are at once tactile and visual, practical and symbolic – the impact of the 'culture' cannot be separated from the impact of functional use. Material civilization is shaped by the objects we interact with. I have argued that sociology needs to attend to the changes in material civilization that have shifted the agenda from Marx's concern with production, via the analysis of consumption to the way that objects affect individual social lives and the life of our society. While the changes that have characterized material civilization in the twentieth century are not each in themselves of great significance, I would suggest that together they amount to a change in society that is as important as the transformation in the class structure or the progress of individualization – but it has hardly been studied.

To engage with the material stuff that surrounds us is to unlock the human agency that has been 'congealed' within it. To interact with objects is to confront our society by releasing their hypostatized cultural content by making them ours, or as Miller puts it: 'Consumption as work may be defined as that which translates the object from an alienable to an inalienable condition' (1987: 190). Theories of consumption have addressed the social significance of the economic act of consumption as a way of symbolically marking class and group boundaries. What they have told us little about is how our everyday routine interactions with the material world shape what it is to be a member of a late modern society. The habitus of the late modern individual is more than ever constituted by material things that are appropriated through the senses and actions of the body. Whereas for previous material civilizations, the material world would have been predominantly 'natural' and the social world was organized to 'dominate' and 'exploit' it, in late modern society the culture of materiality shapes the social world, mediating relations between individuals but most especially those between individuals and the broader society. The rapidity of change in material culture in late modernity means that it transforms far more quickly than languages can evolve, reversing the dominance of older age groups over younger, achieving its impact as much through its practical uses as through its capacity as a vehicle for signification. As children teach their parents how to use the functionality of, say, a mobile phone, they are drawing on an acquired bodily capacity to adapt to objects that have been made from a set of synthetic materials designed for their purpose, that have multiple functionality and aesthetic and ergonomic styling that varies between types. The mobile phone provides an interface between humans but it can substitute for them when they are not there, acting autonomously in accord with how it has been set to answer, record or divert calls. The mobile phone undoubtedly has created practical uses for itself within the everyday lives of many people in ways that could not have been precisely planned or intended by the most prescient engineer/entrepreneur. And yet as an object that has supremely symbolized the changing nature of material civilization, it has also come to be a bearer of signs of social status and worthiness for a wide variety of people.

What the changes in material culture have produced is a society that we confront not so much directly through our interactions with its members or leaders but through our interaction with the material world that surrounds us. As we interact with the objects that we confront everyday in our lives, few of us can any longer claim to be confronting nature – we are confronting the society that has designed and placed those objects around us. It is in these objects that the stable, consistent 'Other' of society is routinely manifest to us, providing the social background against which our warm human and sociable interactions take place. In the western industrialized world we have fashioned the embodied world we live in and in that sense we live in a material society.

Notes

1 The sociality of things

1 The emphasis is in the original in this quotation and in all other quo-
tations throughout the book unless explicitly stated otherwise.
2 La technique du corps incorpore les objets matériels. Une raquette de
tennis, les roues de la bicyclette, la proue du bateau ou les spatules des
skis vont prolonger le corps et devenir des capteurs sensoriels ... Les
objets matériels sont partie prenante de la pratique corporelle.
3 See e.g. Heath 1986; Heath and Luff 2000; Heath et al. 2000; Hindmarsh
and Heath 2000.
4 The project, 'Car Care: The Professional Repair and Maintenance of the
Private Car', was conducted at the University of East Anglia and funded
by ESRC Small Grant No: R00023370. The study involved fieldwork in
five local garages of different sizes and organizational structure over a
period of seven months in 2001/2. The principal form of data gathered
was the video of repair and maintenance work as it proceeded normally;
the research was designed not to interfere with the flow of ordinary
commercial work. For further information, see Dant and Bowles 2002b;
2003.

2 Material civilization

1 'Dialectics, so-called *objective* dialectics, prevails throughout nature, and
so-called subjective dialectics, dialectical thought, is only the reflex of
the movement in opposites which asserts itself everywhere in nature,
and which by the continual conflict of the opposites and their final
merging into one another, or into higher forms, determines the life of
nature' (Engels 1940: 206).

2 'By producing their means of subsistence men are indirectly producing their actual material life' (Marx and Engels 1974: 42).

3 'In the factory we have a lifeless mechanism which is independent of the workers, who are incorporated into it as its living appendages' (Marx 1976: 548).

4 'Their growing wealth, and the relatively diminished number of workers required to produce the means of subsistence, begets both new luxury requirements and the means of satisfying them ... In other words the production of luxuries increases' (Marx 1976: 573).

5 'The need which consumption feels for the object is created by the perception of it. The object of art – like every other product – creates a public which is sensitive to art and enjoys beauty. Production thus not only creates an object for the subject, but also a subject for the object' (Marx 1973: 92).

6 In arguing that 'Marx de-emphasized consumption', Miller refers to this as 'a highly unsatisfactory section' of the *Grundrisse* (1991: 48).

7 See, however, Miller (1991) who discusses these themes from an Hegelian perspective in terms of 'sublation' and 'alienation' and Slater (1997) who focuses on 'alienated needs' and my own discussion of use-value in relation to 'fetishism' (Dant 1999).

8 For a fascinating account of the continuities and discontinuities between Merleau-Ponty's and Bourdieu's theories of practice, see Crossley (2001).

3 Technology and modernity

1 One of the reasons that the study of material interaction discussed in Chapter 6 was undertaken in car repair centres was that the technicians work with the range from simple hand tools, to machine tools, to more or less autonomous tools.

2 The idea that tools and machines are extensions of the bodily and social capacities of human beings is often associated with McLuhan ([1964] 1994) but Mumford was thinking through the cultural consequences of objects as extensions of humans, thirty years earlier.

3 See Ihde (1990: 59–64) for a discussion of the clock in Mumford that connects it to Heidegger's concept of time.

4 Manuals provide information on the amount of time a certain task on a certain car should take, as well as the exact measurements and specifications of components – they are seldom used for 'how-to' knowledge. Most routine tasks that the technicians undertake they are familiar with and while they use a checklist, they do not follow written instructions.

5 In one service chain a sequence for undertaking servicing was established not by the technician, not by the foreman or the manager but by 'head office' – a group of managers representing the company. The

respondent telling us this reported that the sequence changed from time to time; technicians were able to influence the specified sequence of operations by commenting on their experience but were ultimately expected to follow what the company specified. The logic of the sequence attempted to follow scientific principles; by sequencing tasks to fit with the flow of movement around the vehicle, the time and effort to do the job could be reduced.

6 'Safety and order are, to a large extent, guaranteed by the fact that man has learned to adjust his behaviour to the other fellow's down to the most minute detail. All men act equally rationally, that is to say, according to the standards which insure the functioning of the apparatus and thereby the maintenance of their own life' (Marcuse 1998: 51).

7 He defines technique as the '*totality of methods rationally arrived at and having absolute efficiency* (for a given stage of development) in *every* field of activity' (Ellul 1965: xxxiii).

8 '*Technical codes define the object in strictly technical terms in accordance with the social meaning it has acquired*' (Feenberg 1999: 88). Drawing on studies of the history and sociology of technology, Feenberg argues that technical codes are fixed when a particular technology is chosen for development because it meets certain social standards. There are now a number of carefully researched accounts of the social exigencies that led to particular technologies: the safety bicycle (Pinch and Bijker 1987), the electric refrigerator (Schwartz-Cowan 1985), and the gasoline car (Schiffer 2000) are a few.

4 Agency, affordance and actor-networks

1 On peut par example porter des sous-vêtements noirs et des vêtements colorés, ou l'inverse. De même, les matières soyeuses peuvent être tournées entre le corps et les matières rêches dirigées vers l'extérieur, ou le contraire. Enfin, l'amplitude des étoffes du dessus peut recouvrir des vêtements serrés comme un emmaillotage secret. La dynamique du vêtement du dessus – plus 'sociable' – et du vêtement du dessous – plus 'intime' – raconte l'histoire des états émotifs et affectifs de chacun à chaque moment.

2 'La forme spécifique de symbolisation mise en jeu dans le vêtement est d'abord sensori-affective-motrice.'

3 'Certains hommes semblent d'ailleurs passer plus de temps à s'occuper de la carrosserie qui recouvre leur véhicule que de la peau a qui recouvre leur corps.'

4 'Les objets ne sont pas seulement des prolongements de nos organes moteurs ou sensoriels. Ils sont, plus fondamentalement, des prolongements du notre esprit.'

5 Gibson makes clear that he was, to some degree, influenced by the gestalt psychologists including K. Koffka, who were also an influence on Merleau-Ponty (see Chapter 5).
6 For a commentary see McCarthy (1984) and Dant (1999: 120–3).
7 Sharrock and Coulter made the same point in relation to bananas, e-coli bacteria and mothers (1998: 155).
8 Interestingly this has a cultural dimension in that chimps in one area will fashion and use twigs in one way to get at termites while chimps in another area will use the twigs differently for the same purpose; they learn the 'local' material civilization of their group. Whiten and his colleagues identified 39 different 'cultural' behaviours that varied between local groups of chimpanzees (1999).
9 Latour does have some photographs of the Aramis transit system (1996) and a few photographs that are integral to a description of humans interacting with objects in scientific fieldwork (1999).
10 Latour's position is of course precisely in contrast to Weber's discussion of the action of firing a gun where the issue is one of whether we can understand the motive as rational or not – for Weber the status of the gun is not worthy of discussion (1978: 9).

5 Being-with materiality

1 'Dasein' translates literally as 'Being there' with the connotation of referring to the existence of a person (Heidegger 1962: 27, fn1).
2 I am most grateful to Andrea Kenkmann who tried hard to make me see the subtle complexity of Heidegger's use of German – the failure in understanding remains of course mine.
3 As it was for the technicians in the 'Car Care' project – see Chapter 1, note 4.
4 Dreyfus translates *Zuhandenheit* as 'availableness' which is slightly less clumsy and more directly meaningful in English than the usual translation of 'ready-to-hand' (1991: xi).
5 Dreyfus translates *Vorhandenheit* as 'occurrentness' instead of the usual 'presence-at-hand' (1991: xi).
6 Of course the sociologist as a sociologist first appropriates the environment as ready-to-hand by seeing it as a 'setting' in which 'work' proceeds and 'interactions' take place ... and so on.
7 See Chapter 6, Figure 6.8.
8 See Chapter 6, Figures 6.10 and 6.14.
9 Dreyfus translates Heidegger's wordplay *Ent-fernung* as 'dis-stance' rather than 'de-severance' which he regards as 'unnecessarily strange' (1991: xi).

10 Unlike Heidegger whose work is resolutely philosophical, Merleau-Ponty's writing engages with debates in clinical psychology and elsewhere in his writing with matters of politics, culture – especially language – and society. John O'Neill (1970, 1985) has for some time been pointing out how Merleau-Ponty's phenomenology can contribute to sociological understanding and more recently Nick Crossley (2001) has explored his analysis of embodiment in relation to identity, desire and habit.

11 There are other limits to the ability of animals to achieve the connection between perception and action that is normal for humans. Merleau-Ponty discusses Koehler's studies with chimpanzees that identify their limitations in terms of linking perceptions to action and things: for example, while good at balancing themselves they are not good at balancing things (1983: 113–20).

12 Body awareness – Merleau-Ponty uses the term to distinguish his conception from psychological versions of body image that see it as a product of sensory information (1962: 99).

13 Writing in French, Merleau-Ponty plays on the double meaning of the word *sens* which translates not only as 'sense' but also as 'meaning' – it can also translate as 'direction' or 'way' and Merleau-Ponty also sometimes uses this third dimension of meaning in the word.

14 Sartre makes a similar point (1991: 9–10).

15 'I perceive a thing because I have a field of existence and because each phenomenon, on its appearance, attracts towards that field the whole of my body as a system of perceptual powers' (Merleau-Ponty 1962: 318).

16 The term is borrowed from Husserl and refers to a field's double dimension: 'the here-there dimension and the past-present-future dimension' (Merleau-Ponty 1962: 265).

17 Don Ihde extends the idea of embodied feeling through the car with the example of parallel parking (1990: 74).

18 'every perception is a communication or a communion, the taking up or completion by us of some extraneous intention or, on the other hand, the complete expression outside ourselves of our perceptual powers and a coition, so to speak, of our body with things' (Merleau-Ponty 1962: 320).

6 Material interaction

1 'Les objets sont pour nous, souvent sans que nous nous en rendions compte, les compagnons de nos actions, de nos émotions et de nos pensées. Ils ne nous accompagnent pas seulement du berceau à tombe. Ils nous précèdeent dans l'un et nous survivent dans l'autre. Demain ils parleront notre langue. Mais ne nous parlent-ils pas déjà, et parfois bien mieux qu'avec des mots?'

2 It seems that the ease and frequency with which ordinary things 'talk' to those with special tools to understand them is likely to increase; Dyson have invented a vacuum cleaner that can 'speak' to the engineer down a telephone about its origins and its problems (Gibbs 2003).

3 There is too an emerging strand of cultural analysis which emphasizes the emotional rather than symbolic aspect of embodiment and interaction – see Csordas's interesting collection (1994).

4 Barthes of course argues that all objects have a symbolic meaning because they are produced and consumed. He suggests that even the glass of water on his podium (an object that might aspire to the degree zero of pure functionality) has the signifying function of identifying its user as the lecturer (1993: 66).

5 See Chapter 1, especially note 4.

6 During the project we saw no making of parts from scratch and very little complex engineering. Most of the work consisted of identifying defective or worn-out components and replacing them.

7 Mead (1980: 119–39); see also McCarthy (1984), and Dant (1999: 121–3). See also Schutz and Luckmanns' incorporation of the idea of a 'manipulative zone' from Mead into their 'zone of operation' in which direct action takes place, (1974: 41–2).

8 'The meaning of a thing for a person grows out of the ways in which other persons act toward the person with regard to the thing. Their actions operate to define the thing for the person' (Blumer 1969a: 4).

9 A visitor refers to the length of pipe as Ray's 'persuader', punning on the use of iron bars by violent people to persuade others to comply with their wishes.

10 In other garages equipped with lifts rather than pits, we saw this task being undertaken with the technician standing and working in a larger field.

11 See Goodwin (1994) and Hindmarsh and Heath (2000) for an analytical approach to gaze in relation to objects and interaction between people.

12 Within the brackets are pauses; '.' indicates a minimal pause of less than two tenths of a second, a figure indicates the length of pauses in seconds – see Heath and Luff (2000: 27).

13 Replacement exhaust pipes, made of extruded and bent metal, come in sections to make fitting easier but they are easily damaged in storage and transit. The result is that they often need some 'coaxing' to fit.

14 Julian Orr's (1996) ethnographic study of the work of repairing photocopier machines demonstrates that dealing with contingencies creates a complex work environment that requires a range of skills but his focus is on the interaction between relatively isolated workers and how they solve their problems. Kusterer (1978) offers some case-study interview evidence to suggest that production work is in fact not simply mechan-

ical and its workers require specific 'know-how' if it is to keep going. His argument goes little further than making a case for recognizing the skill base of so-called 'unskilled' workers. Neither of these studies address the embodied nature of material interaction.

7 Materiality and society

1   Baudrillard explored the increasing embeddedness of intended functionality within objects in 1968 – the 'gadget' is marked by its multifunctionality while the mechanizing of function, such as the starter motor which replaces the starter handle, generates a monofunctionality (Baudrillard 1996).
2   It is the emergent interconnection of objects, systems and techniques that Shove (2003) calls 'co-evolution'.

Bibliography

Adams, J. (1999) *The Social Implications of Hypermobility*. Report for OECD Project on Environmentally Sustainable Transport, *ENV/EPOC/PPC/T(99)3/FINAL*, Paris: OECD.

Akrich, M. (1992) The de-scription of technical objects, in W. Bijker and J. Law (eds) *Shaping Technology, Building Society: Studies in Sociotechnical Change*. Cambridge, MA: MIT Press: 205–24.

Akrich, M. and Latour, B. (1992) A summary of a convenient vocabulary for the semiotics of human and nonhuman assemblies, in W. Bijker and J. Law (eds) *Shaping Technology, Building Society: Studies in Sociotechnical Change*. Cambridge, MA: MIT Press: 259–64.

Barthes, R. ([1957] 1979) *The Eiffel Tower and Other Mythologies*. New York: Hill and Wang.

Barthes, R. ([1967] 1990) *The Fashion System*. Berkeley, CA: University of California Press.

Barthes, R. ([1957] 1993) *Mythologies*. London: Vintage Books.

Barthes, R. (1993) Mythologies de l'automobile [1963], *Œuvres Complètes* Vol. 1: *1942–1965*, Paris: Editions du Seuil.

Baudrillard, J. ([1972] 1981) *For a Critique of the Political Economy of the Sign*. St Louis: Telos Press.

Baudrillard, J. ([1968] 1996) *The System of Objects*. London: Verso.

Baudrillard, J. ([1970] 1998) *The Consumer Society*. London: Sage.

Beynon, H. (1973) *Working for Ford*. Harmondsworth: Allen Lane.

Bijker, W.E., Hughes, T.P. and Pinch, T.J. (eds) (1987) *The Social Construction of Technological Systems*. Cambridge, MA: MIT Press.

Bijker, W. and Law, J. (eds) (1992) *Shaping Technology, Building Society: Studies in Sociotechnical Change*. Cambridge, MA: MIT Press.

Birdwhistell, R.L. (1973) *Kinesics and Context: Essays on Body-Motion Communication*. Harmondsworth: Penguin.

Blumer, H. (1969a) *Symbolic Interactionism: Perspective and Method*. Berkeley, CA: University of California Press.

Blumer, H. (1969b) Fashion: from class differentiation to social selection. *Sociological Quarterly*, 10: 275–91.

Bourdieu, P. (1973) The Berber house, in M. Douglas (ed.) *Rules and Meanings: The Anthropology of Everyday Knowledge*. Harmondsworth: Penguin Education.

Bourdieu, P. ([1979] 1984) *Distinction: A Social Critique of the Judgement of Taste*. London: Routledge.

Bourdieu, P. ([1980] 1990) *The Logic of Practice*. Stanford, CA: Stanford University Press.

Bowles, D. and Dant, T. (2002) Dirty work: fixing cars for us. Paper presented to the British Sociological Association, University of Leicester, 25–27 March 2002.

Braudel, F. ([1979] 1982) *The Wheels of Commerce*. London: Collins.

Braudel, F. ([1979] 1992) *The Structures of Everyday Life: The Limits of the Possible*. Berkeley, CA: University of California Press.

Brenna, B., Law, J. and Moser, I. (eds) (1998) *Machines, Agency and Desire*. Oslo: Centre for Technology and Culture.

Brewer, J. and Porter, R. (eds) (1993) *Consumption and the World of Goods*. London: Routledge.

Bruun, H. and Langlais, R. (2003) On the embodied nature of action, *Acta Sociologica*, 46(1): 31–49.

Burke, P. (1990) *The French Historical Revolution: The* Annales *School, 1929–89*. Cambridge: Polity Press.

Callon, M. (1986a) The sociology of an actor-network: the case of the electric vehicle, in M. Callon, J. Law and A. Rip (eds) *Mapping the Dynamics of Science and Technology: Sociology of Science in the Real World*. Basingstoke: Macmillan.

Callon, M. (1986b) Some elements of a sociology of translation: domestication of the scallops and the fishermen of Saint Brieuc Bay, in J. Law (ed.) *Power, Action and Belief: a new Sociology of Knowledge?* London, Routledge and Kegan Paul. 32: 196–233.

Callon, M. (1987) Society in the making: the study of technology as a tool for sociological analysis, in W.E. Bijker, T.P. Hughes and T.J. Pinch (eds) *The Social Construction of Technical Systems: New Directions in the Sociology and History of Technology*. Cambridge, MA: MIT Press: 83–103.

Callon, M. (1991) Techno-economic networks and irreversibility, in J. Law (ed.) *A Sociology of Monsters: Essays on Power, Technology and Domination*. London: Routledge.

Callon, M., Law, J. and Rip, A. (eds) (1986) *Mapping the Dynamics of Science and Technology: Sociology of Science in the Real World*. Basingstoke: Macmillan.

Campbell, C. (1989) *The Romantic Ethic and the Spirit of Modern Capitalism*. Oxford: Blackwell.

Certeau, M. de, Giard, L. and Mayol, P. ([1980] 1998) *The Practice of Everday Life*, Vol. 2: *Living and Cooking*. Minneapolis: Minnesota Press.

Certeau, M. de ([1974] 1984) *The Practice of Everyday Life*. Berkeley, CA: University of California Press.

Chinoy, E. (1955) *Automobile Workers and the American Dream*. Boston: Beacon.

Corrigan, P. (1997) *The Sociology of Consumption: An Introduction*. London: Sage.

Cosgrove, W.J. and Rijsberman, F.R. (2000) *World Water Vision: Making Water Everybody's Business*. London: Earthscan Publications Ltd.

Costall, A. (1995) Socializing Affordances, *Theory and Psychology*, 5(4): 467–81.

Costall, A. (1997) The Meaning of Things, *Social Analysis*, 41(1): 76–85.

Crossley, N. (2001) *The Social Body: Habit, Identity and Desire*. London: Sage.

Csordas, T.J. (ed.) (1994) *Embodiment and Experience: The Existential Ground of Culture and Self*. Cambridge: Cambridge University Press.

Dant, T. (1998) Playing with things: objects and subjects in windsurfing, *Journal of Material Culture*, 3(1): 77–95.

Dant, T. (1999) *Material Culture in the Social World: Values, Activities, Lifestyles*. Buckingham: Open University Press.

Dant, T. (2000a) Driving identities. Paper presented at Mobilizing forces: Social and Cultural Aspects of Automobility Conference, Göteborg, Sweden.

Dant, T. (2000b) Consumption caught in the cash nexus, *Sociology*, 34(4): 655–70.

Dant, T. (2001) Fruitbox/toolbox: biography and objects, *Auto/Biography*. IX(1–2): 11–20.

Dant, T. (2004) The driver-car, *Theory, Culture and Society*, 21(4).

Dant, T. and Bowles, D. (2002a) Things talk back: material interaction with cars during their repair. Paper presented to 'Automobility' conference, Keele University, September 2002.

Dant, T. and Bowles, D. (2002b) *Car Care: The Professional Repair and Maintenance of the Private Car*. Summary Final Report mimeo, University of East Anglia.

Dant, T. and Bowles, D. (2003) Dealing with dirt: servicing and repairing cars' *Sociological Research Online*, 8(2), *http://www.socresonline.org.uk/8/2/dant.html*.

Dant, T. and Martin, P.J. (2001) By car: carrying modern society, in A. Warde and J. Grunow (eds) *Ordinary Consumption*. London: Routledge.

DETR (2000) *Transport Statistics Great Britain 2000*, 26th Edition. London: HMSO.

Dodson, S. (2003) The internet of things, *The Guardian*. Thursday, 9 October 2003.

Douglas, M. and Isherwood, B. (1979) *The World of Goods: Towards an Anthropology of Consumption.* London: Routledge.

Dreyfus, H. (1991) *Being-in-the-World: A Commentary on Heidegger's* Being and Time. *Division 1.* Cambridge, MA: MIT Press.

Durkheim, E. ([1893] 1933) *The Division of Labour in Society.* New York: Free Press.

Elias, N. (1995) Technization and civilization, *Theory, Culture and Society.* 12(3): 7–42.

Ellul, J. ([1954] 1965) *The Technological Society.* London: Jonathan Cape.

Engels, F. ([1845]) *The Conditions of the Working-Class in England in 1844.* Oxford: Blackwell.

Engels, F. (1936) *Anti-Dühring.* London: Lawrence and Wishart.

Engels, F. (1940) *Dialectics of Nature.* London: Lawrence and Wishart.

Farnell, B.M. (1994) Ethno-graphics and the moving body, *Man,* 29(4): 929–94.

Feenberg, A. (1991) *The Critical Theory of Technology.* New York: Oxford University Press.

Feenberg, A. (1999) *Questioning Technology.* London: Routledge.

Feenberg, A. (2002) *Transforming Technology: A Critical Theory Revisited.* Oxford University Press.

Flink, J. (1975) *Car Culture.* Cambridge, MA: MIT Press.

Flink, J. (1988) *The Automobile Age.* Cambridge, MA: MIT Press.

Forty, A. (1990) Design and mechanization: the standardized product, in C. Pirovano (ed.) *History of Industrial Design: 1815–1918, The Great Emporium of the World.* Milan: Electra.

Gartman, D. (1994) *Auto Opium: A Social History of American Automobile Design.* London: Routledge.

Gell, A. (1998) *Art and Agency: An Anthropological Theory.* Oxford: Clarendon Press.

Gibbs, G. (2003) Dyson develops vacuum cleaner that can talk, *The Guardian.* Tuesday, 7 October 2003.

Gibson, J.J. (1968) *The Senses Considered as Perceptual Systems.* London: George, Allen & Unwin.

Gibson, J.J. (1979) *The Ecological Approach to Visual Perception.* Boston: Houghton Mifflin.

Gibson, J.J. ([1938] 1982a) A theoretical field-analysis of automobile driving, in E. Reed and R. Jones (eds) *Reasons for Realism: Selected Essays of James J. Gibson.* Hillsdale, NJ: Lawrence Erlbaum Associates.

Gibson, J.J. ([1947] 1982b) The ability to judge distance and space in terms of retinal motion cue, in E. Reed and R. Jones (eds) *Reasons for Realism: Selected Essays of James J. Gibson.* Hillsdale, NJ: Lawrence Erlbaum Associates.

Giddens, A. (1991) *Modernity and Self-Identity.* Cambridge: Polity Press.

Gilloch, G. and Dant, T. (2004) From *'Passage'* to *'Parly 2'*: commodity culture in Benjamin and Baudrillard. *New Formations*

Goffman, E. (1971) *Relations in Public: Microstudies of the Public Order.* New York: Basic Books.

Goldthorpe, J.H., Lockwood, D., Bechhofer, F. and Platt, J. (1968) *The Affluent Worker: (1) Industrial Attitudes and Behaviour and (2) Political Attitudes and Behaviour.* Cambridge: Cambridge University Press.

Goodwin, C. (1994) Professional vision, *American Anthropologist*, 96(3): 606–33.

Grint, K. and Woolgar, S. (1997) *Machine at Work.* Cambridge: Polity Press.

Hardt, M. and Negri, A. (1999) *Empire.* Cambridge, MA: Harvard University Press.

Hawkin, P., Lovins, A.B. and Lovins, L.H. (1999) *Natural Capitalism: The Next Industrial Revolution.* London: Earthscan Publications.

Hawkins, R. (1986) A road not taken: sociology and the neglect of the automobile', *California Sociologist*, 9(1–2): 61–79.

Heath, C. (1986) *Body Movement and Speech in Medical Interaction.* Cambridge: Cambridge University Press.

Heath, C., Knoblauch, H. and Luff, P. (2000) Technology and social interaction: the emergence of 'workplace studies', *British Journal of Sociology*, 51(2): 299–320.

Heath, C. and Luff, P. (2000) *Technology in Action.* Cambridge: Cambridge University Press.

Heidegger, M. ([1927; 1931; 1957] 1962) *Being and Time.* Oxford: Blackwell.

Heidegger, M. (1977a) The question concerning technology, in *The Question Concerning Technology and Other Essays.* New York: Harper Row.

Heidegger, M. (1977b) The turning, in *The Question Concerning Technology and Other Essays.* New York: Harper Row.

Hill, S. (1988) *The Tragedy of Technology.* London: Pluto Press.

Hindmarsh, J. and Heath, C. (2000) Sharing the tools of the trade, *Journal of Contemporary Ethnography*, 29(5): 523–63.

Horkheimer, M. (1947) *Eclipse of Reason.* New York: Oxford University Press.

Horkheimer, M. (1974) *Critique of Instrumental Reason.* New York: The Seabury Press.

Horkheimer, M. (1999) *Critical Theory: Selected Essays.* New York: Continuum.

Howes, D. (2003) *Sensual Relations: Engaging the Senses in Culture and Social Theory.* Ann Arbor, MI: University of Michigan Press.

Hughes, T.P. (1983) *Networks of Power: Electrification in Western Society 1880–1930.* Baltimore, MD: Johns Hopkins University Press.

Hughes, T.P. (1987) The evolution of large technological systems, in W. Bijker, T. Hughes and T. Pinch (eds) *The Social Construction of Technological Systems.* Cambridge, MA: MIT Press.

Hughes, T.P. (1999) Edison and electric light, in D. MacKenzie and J. Wajcman (eds) *The Social Shaping of Technology*. 2nd edition. Buckingham: Open University Press.

Hutchby, I. (2001) Technologies, texts and affordances, *Sociology*, 35(2): 441–56.

Ihde, D. (1974) The experience of technology: human-machine relations, *Cultural Hermeneutics*, 2: 267–79.

Ihde, D. (1990) *Technology of the Lifeworld: From Garden to Earth*. Bloomington: Indiana University Press.

Knorr-Cetina, K. (1997) Sociality with objects: social relations in postsocial knowledge societies, *Theory Culture and Society*, 14(4): 1–30.

Kusterer, K.C. (1978) *Know-How on the Job: The Important Working Knowledge of Unskilled Workers*. Boulder, CO: Westview Press.

Lahire, B. (1998) *L' Homme pluriel*. Paris: Nathan.

Latour, B. (1988a) *The Pasturization of France*. Cambridge, MA: Harvard University Press.

Latour, B. (1988b) Mixing humans and nonhumans together: the sociology of a door-closer, *Social Problems*, 35(3): 298–310.

Latour, B. (1991) Technology is society made durable, in J. Law (ed.) *A Sociology of Monsters: Essays on Power, Technology and Domination*. London: Routledge.

Latour, B. (1992a) Where are the missing masses? The sociology of a few mundane artifacts, in W. Bijker and J. Law (eds) *Shaping Technology, Building Society: Studies in Sociotechnical Change*. Cambridge, MA: MIT Press.

Latour, B. (1992b) Sociology of a few mundane artifacts, in W. Bijker and J. Law (eds) *Shaping Technology, Building Society: Studies in Sociotechnical Change*. Cambridge, MA: MIT Press.

Latour, B. (1996) *Aramis or the Love of Technology*. Cambridge, MA: Harvard University Press.

Latour, B. (1999) *Pandora's Hope: Essays on the Reality of Science Studies*. Cambridge, MA: Harvard University Press.

Laurier, Eric (2004) Doing officework on the motorway, *Theory, Culture and Society*, 21(4).

Law, J. (ed.) (1991) *A Sociology of Monsters: Essays on Power, Technology and Domination*. London: Routledge.

Law, J. and Callon, M. (1992) The life and death of an aircraft: A network analysis of technical change', in W. Bijker and J. Law (eds) *Shaping Technology, Building Society: Studies in Sociotechnical Change*. Cambridge, MA: MIT Press.

Law, J. and Mol, A. (1995) Notes on materiality and sociality, *Sociological Review*, 43(2): 274–94.

Lefebvre, H. ([1968] 1971) *Everyday Life in the Modern World*. London: Allen Lane.

Lefebvre, H. ([1947/58] 1991a) *Critique of Everyday Life:* Vol. I. London: Verso.

Lefebvre, H. (1991b) *The Production of Space.* Oxford: Blackwells.

Lefebvre, H. ([1961] 2002) *Critique of Everyday Life:* Vol. II. *Foundations for a Sociology of the Everyday.* London: Verso.

Loscerbo, J. (1981) *Being and Technology: A Sudy in the Philosophy of Martin Heidegger.* The Hague: Martinus Nijhoff.

Luff, P., Hindmarsh, J. and Heath, C. (2000) *Workplace Studies: Recovering Work Practice and Informing System Design.* Cambridge: Cambridge University Press.

MacKenzie, D. and Wajcman, J. (eds) (1985) *The Social Shaping of Technology: A Reader.* Milton Keynes: Open University Press.

Malinowski, B. (1922) *Argonauts of the Western Pacific.* London: Routledge and Kegan Paul.

Marcuse, H. (1978) *The Aesthetic Dimension: Toward a Critique of Marxist Aesthetics.* London and Basingstoke: Macmillan.

Marcuse, H. ([1964] 1991) *One-Dimensional Man: Studies in the Ideology of Advanced Industrial Society.* London: Routledge.

Marcuse, H. ([1941] 1998) Some social implications of modern technology, in H. Marcuse, *Technology, War and Fascism.* London: Routledge.

Marrow, A.J. (1969) *The Practical Theorist: The Life and Work of Kurt Lewin.* New York: Basic Books.

Marx, K. (1970) *A Contribution to the Critique of Political Economy.* London: Lawrence and Wishart.

Marx, K. (1973) *Grundrisse.* Harmondsworth: Penguin Books.

Marx, K. (1974) *Capital,* Vol Three. London: Lawrence and Wishart.

Marx, K. (1975) *Early Writings.* London: Penguin.

Marx, K. (1976) *Capital* Volume One. London: Penguin Books.

Marx, K. and Engels, F. (1974) *The German Ideology.* London: Lawrence and Wishart.

Mauss, M. ([1934] 1973) Techniques of the body, *Economy and Society,* 2(1): 70–88.

Mauss, M.([1950] 1990) *The Gift: The Form and Reason for Exchange in Archaic Societies.* London: Routledge.

McCarthy, E.D. (1984) Toward a sociology of the physical world: George Herbert Mead on physical objects, *Studies in Symbolic Interaction,* 5: 105–21.

McCracken, G. (1988) *Culture and Consumption.* Bloomington and Indianapolis: Indiana University Press.

McKendrick, N., Brewer, J. and Plumb, J.H. (1983) *The Birth of a Consumer Society.* London: Hutchinson.

McLuhan, M. ([1964] 1994) *Understanding Media: The Extensions of Man.* Cambridge, MA: MIT Press.

Mead, G.H. ([1934] 1962) *Mind, Self, and Society: From the Standpoint of a Social Behaviorist.* Edited by Charles W. Morris, Chicago: University of Chicago Press.

Mead, G.H. ([1932] 1980) *Philosophy of the Present.* Chicago: University of Chicago Press.

Merleau-Ponty, M. ([1945] 1962) *Phenomenology of Perception.* London: Routledge.

Merleau-Ponty, M. ([1961] 1964a) Eye and mind, in *The Primacy of Perception.* Evanston, IL: Northwestern University Press.

Merleau-Ponty, M. ([1960] 1964b) From Mauss to Claude Lévi-Strauss, in *Signs.* Evanston, IL: Northwestern University Press.

Merleau-Ponty, M. (1974) The philosopher and sociology, in *Phenomenology, Language and Sociology.* London: Heinemann Educational Books.

Merleau-Ponty, M. ([1942] 1983) *The Structure of Behaviour.* Pittsburgh: Duquesne University Press.

Miller, D. (1987) *Material Culture and Mass Consumption.* Oxford: Blackwell.

Miller, D. (1997) Consumption and its consequences, in H. Mackay (ed.) *Consumption and Everyday Life.* London: Sage (in association with The Open University Press).

Miller, D. (2001a) Driven societies, in D. Miller (ed.) *Car Cultures.* Oxford: Berg.

Miller, D. (ed.) (2001b) *Car Cultures.* Oxford: Berg.

Mintel (2002) *Car Servicing/MOT.* February, Mintel International Group Limited.

Molotch, H. (2003) *Where Stuff Comes From: How Toaster, Toilets, Cars, Computers, and Many Other Things Come to Be as They Are.* New York: Routledge.

Motavalli, J. (2000) *Forward Drive: The Race to Build Clean Cars for the Future.* San Francisco: The Sierra Club Books.

Mumford, L. (1934) *Technics and Civilization.* London: Routledge.

Mumford, L. (1967) *The Myth of the Machine: Technics and Human Development.* London: Secker & Warburg.

O'Connell, S. (1998) *The Car and British Society: Class, Gender and Motoring, 1896–1939.* Manchester: Manchester University Press.

O'Neill, J. (1970) *Perception, Expression and History: The Social Phenomenology of Maurice Merleau-Ponty.* Evanston, IL: Northwestern University Press.

O'Neill, J. (1985) *Five Bodies: The Human Shape of Modern Society.* Ithaca, NY: Cornell University Press.

Orr, J.E. (1996) *Talking About Machines: An Ethnography of a Modern Job.* Ithaca, NY: Cornell University Press.

Parlebas, P. (1999) Les Tactique du corps, in M-P Julien and J-P Warnier (eds) *Approches de la culture matérielle.* Paris: L'Harmattan.

Pels, D., Hetherington, K. and Vandenberghe, F. (eds) (2002) special issue on Materiality, *Theory, Culture and Society,* 19 (15–16).

Pinch, T. and Bijker, W. (1987) The social construction of facts and artifacts: or how the sociology of science and the sociology of technology might benefit each other, in W. Bijker, T. Hughes and T. Pinch (eds) *The Social Construction of Technological Systems: New Directions in the Sociology and History of Technology*. Cambridge, MA: The MIT Press.

Preda, A. (1999) The turn to things: arguments for a sociological theory of things, *Sociological Quarterly*, 40(2): 342–67.

Roche, D. (2000) *A History of Everyday Things*. Cambridge: Cambridge University Press.

Sachs, W. (1992) *For Love of the Automobile: Looking Back into the History of Our Desires*. Berkeley, CA: University of California Press.

Sahlins, M. (1976) *Culture and Practical Reason*. Chicago: University of Chicago Press.

Sartre, J-P. (1984) *Being and Nothingness*. New York: Washington Square Books.

Sartre, J-P. (1991) *The Psychology of Imagination*. New York: Citadel Press.

Schiffer, M. (2000) Indigenous theories, scientific theories and product histories, in P. Graves-Brown (ed.) *Matter, Materiality and Modern Culture*. London: Routledge.

Schiffer, M.B. (1999) *The Material Life of Human Beings*. London: Routledge.

Schön, D.A. (1967) *Technology and Change*. Oxford: Pergamon Press.

Schutz, A. and Luckmann, T. (1974) *The Structures of the Life-World*. London: Heinemann.

Schwartz-Cowan, E. (1985) How the refrigerator got its hum, in D. McKenzie and J. Wajcman (eds) *The Social Shaping of Technology*. Buckingham: Open University Press.

Sharrock, W. and Coulter, J. (1998) On what we can see, *Theory and Psychology*, 8(2): 147–64.

Shove, E. (2003) *Comfort, Cleanliness and Convenience: The Social Organisation of Normality*. Oxford: Berg.

Simmel, G. (1950) *The Sociology of Georg Simmel*. Edited by Kurt H. Wolff, Glencoe, IL.: Free Press.

Simmel, G. (1971a) *On Individuality and Social Forms: Selected Writings*. Edited by Donald N. Levine, Chicago: University of Chicago Press.

Simmel, G. ([1904] 1971b) Fashion, in G. Simmel, *On Individuality and Social Forms: Selected Writings*. Edited by Donald N. Levine, Chicago: University of Chicago Press.

Simmel, G. (1990) *The Philosophy of Money*. London: Routledge.

Slater, D. (1997) *Consumer Culture and Modernity*. Cambridge: Polity.

Sudnow, D. (2001) *Ways of the Hand: A Rewritten Account*. Cambridge, MA: MIT Press.

Thompson, M. (1979) *Rubbish Theory: The Creation and Destruction of Value*. Oxford: Oxford University Press.

Thoms, D., Holden, L. and Claydon, T. (eds) (1998) *The Motor Car and Popular Culture in the 20th Century*. Aldershot: Ashgate.

Thurk, J. and Fine, G.A. (2003) The problem of tools: technology and the sharing of knowledge, *Acta Sociologica*, 46(2): 107–17.

Tisseron, S. (1999) *Comment l'esprit vient aux objets*. Paris: Aubier.

Urry, J. (1999) Automobility, car culture and weightless travel: a discussion paper. Department of Sociology, Lancaster University, http://www.lancaster.ac.uk/sociologysoc008ju.html.

Urry, J. (2000) *Sociology Beyond Society*. London: Sage.

Veblen, T. (1925) *The Theory of the Leisure Class: An Economic Study of Institutions*. London: George Allen & Unwin.

Veblen, T. ([1895] 1964a) The economic theory of woman's dress, in *Essays in our Changing Order*. New York: Augustus M. Kelly and the Sentry Press.

Veblen, T. ([1914] 1964b) *The Instinct of Workmanship: and the State of the Industrial Arts*. New York: Augustus M. Kelly and the Sentry Press.

Verrips, J. and Meyer, B. (2001) Kwaku's car: the struggles and stories of a Ghanaian long-distance taxi-driver, in D. Miller (ed.) *Car Cultures*. Oxford: Berg.

Warnier, J-P. (2001) A praxaeological approach to subjectivation in a material world, *Journal of Material Culture*. 6(1): 5–24.

Warnier, J-P. and Julien, M-P. (1999) *Approches de la culture de la matérielle*. Paris: L'Harmattan.

Weber, M, ([1921] 1978) *Economy and Society*. eds Guenther Roth and Claus Wittich, Berkeley, CA: University of California Press.

Whiteley, N. (1993) *Design for Society*. London: Reaktion Books.

Whiten, A., Goodall, J., McGrew, W.C., Nishida, T., Reynolds, V., Sugiyama, Y., Tutin, C.E.G., Wrangham, R.W. and Boesch, C. (1999) Cultures in chimpanzees, *Nature*, 399: 682–5.

Winner, L. (1977) *Autonomous Technology: Technics-out-of-Control as a Theme in Political Thought*. Cambridge, MA: The MIT Press.

Index